The Heretical Political Discourse

– a Discourse Analysis of the Danish Debate on Basic Income

Erik Christensen

AALBORG UNIVERSITY PRESS
2008

The Heretical Political Discourse
– a Discourse Analysis of the Danish Debate on Basic Income
Erik Christensen

© The Author and Aalborg University Press, 2008

Cover & Layout: Lars Pedersen / Anblik Grafisk

Printed by Publizon A/S
ISBN-13: 978-87-7307-936-2

Distribution:
Aalborg University Press
Niels Jernes Vej 6B
9220 Aalborg
Denmark
Phone: (+45) 99 40 71 40, Fax: (+45) 96 35 00 76
E-mail: aauf@forlag.aau.dk

www.forlag.aau.dk

All rights reserved. No part of this book may be reprinted or reproduced or utilized in any form or by any electronic, mechanical, or other means, now known or hereafter invented, including photocopying and recording, or in any information storage or retrieval system, without permission in writing from the publishers, except for reviews and short excerpts in scholarly publications.

Contents

	Acknowledgements	5
	Introduction	7
1.	Citizen's Income as a Heretical Political Discourse: the Danish Debate about Citizen's Income	19
2.	The Rhetoric of Rights and Obligations in Denmark from a Labour History Perspective	45
3.	Feminist Arguments in Favour of Welfare and Basic Income in Denmark	63
4.	Welfare Discourses in Denmark from a Basic Income Perspective	91
5.	A Global Ecological Argument for a Basic Income	119
6.	Basic Income on the Political Agenda: between Inclusion and Exclusion	139
	References	147

Acknowledgements

Chapter 1 was originally published as a working paper from the Department of Economics, Politics and Public Administration, Aalborg University, 1998:2, and later in *Inclusion and Exclusion: Unemployment and non-standard Employment in Europe*, edited by Jens Lind and Iver Hornemann Møller, 1999, Ashgate, (ISBN 978-1-84014-849-7). p. 13-33, and it is here reprinted in a slightly revised version by kind permission of Jens Lind, Iver Hornemann Møller and Ashgate Publishing Ltd.

Chapter 2 was first presented as a paper at the 8th International Congress on Basic Income, Berlin, October 6-7, 2000 and later as a working paper from the Department of Economics, Politics and Public Administration, Aalborg University, 2001:3.

Chapter 3 was originally presented as a paper at the 9th International Congress on Basic Income, Geneva, September 12 –14, 2002. Later it was published as a working paper from the Department of Economics, Politics and Public Administration, Aalborg University 2003:2, and as an revised article in Guy Standing (ed.) *Promoting Income Security as a Right: Europe and North America*. London: Anthem Press 2004. p. 382-400. This article is here reprinted by kind permission of ILO, Copyright © 2005 International Labour Organization.

Chapter 4 was first presented as a paper at the 10th International Congress on Basic Income, Barcelona, September 19 -21, 2004, and later as a working paper from the Department of Economics, Politics and Public Administration, Aalborg University, 2005:7.

Chapter 5 is a translation of an article: 'En global økologisk begrundelse for borgerløn' from the Scandinavian basic income anthology: Erik Christensen, Karsten Lieberkind and Christian Ydesen (red.) *Retten til basisindkomst. En demokratisk frigørelse.* Göteborg : Nordic Summer University Press, 2007.

Chapter 6 is also a translation of an article: 'Basisindkomst på den politiske dagsorden – mellem inklusion og eksklusion' from the same basic income anthology. NSU Press has kindly accepted the use of chapter 5 and 6 in this anthology.

I would like to express my thanks to Karsten Lieberkind for having revised all the articles, for his linguistic help with the translation into English and for his thoughtful comments and ideas on the composition of the anthology and Jørgen Goul Andersen, Jens Lind, Jørn Loftager and Niels I. Meyer for information on basic income literature about Denmark in English.

Without financial support from my Department of Economics, Politics and Public Administration this anthology could not have been published, and therefore also my thanks to the Department.

I thank the publishing company, Hovedland, for permission to use the cover from my Danish book: *Borgerløn. Fortællinger om en politisk idé.* Århus: Hovedland 2000.

Needless to say, of course, the full responsibility for the finished product is mine alone.

Erik Christensen
Aalborg, May 2008.

Introduction

A basic income is an income unconditionally granted to all on an individual basis, without means test or work requirement.[1]

This anthology about the basic income debate in Denmark consists of a number of articles and papers I have written to two anthologies and to BIEN (Basic Income European Network)[2] congresses since 1998. They show where and how basic income has been part of the Danish welfare discussion.

The first article presents an overview of the history of the Danish debate on basic income and a summary of the book I published in Danish in 2000 on the debate on basic income in Denmark: Erik Christensen: *Borgerløn. Fortællinger om en politisk idé*, 2000 (*Basic Income. Narratives about a Political Idea*).

The next three articles analyse the workfare and feminist discourses in the Danish debate on welfare and basic income: How did the labour movement come to adopt the new workfare strategy and exclude the basic income strategy? What was the women's movement's position in the debate on basic income? And which

---

1 I use the most common term, basic income, in spite of the fact that I used the term citizen's income in my first article. Previously the term citizen's income was chosen because the most common term in Danish is 'borgerløn' ('citizen's wage'), a term used in the famous book *Revolt from the Centre*, Meyer et al. 1982.
2 Basic Income European Network changed its name to Basic Income Earth Network in 2004.

social science paradigms favour the new welfare/workfare policy and exclude the basic income perspective?

These articles are followed by an article providing a global ecological argument for a basic income. The last article discusses a few general conditions for bringing back the basic income question on the political agenda.

The collected articles present a picture of how the Danish welfare state, from the beginning of the 1990s, has evolved from a universal welfare state to a workfare state.

THE THEORETICAL PERSPECTIVE

The common framework for the articles is a discourse-analytical perspective inspired by Norman Fairclough (1992) with analysis of metaphors, narratives and key concepts in welfare analysis (right/obligations, dependence/independence, equality/difference, commodification/decommodification and reciprocity).

A political discourse is defined as a framework of understanding for action for political actors. The main function of a political discourse is to create understanding and support from actors for certain political solutions to the exclusion of other undesired solutions. It is a process of inclusion and exclusion of discourses out of which, in the end, a hegemonic discourse evolves. Hence, political discourses can only be understood in relation to other discourses, and in the same way the basic income discourse in the early 1990s can only be understood in relation to the new activation or workfare discourse at that time.

Society may be seen as a hegemonic community, held together by a hegemonic political discourse. This discourse reproduces and transforms society in an antagonistic interplay with other discourses.

In general, politics deals with the articulation of specific interests and the exclusion of rival interests. As a rule, it is only by creating alliances between actors, by establishing a hegemonic project, that social power can be maintained. And a hegemonic project must be supported by a hegemonic discourse.

WHY IS BASIC INCOME AN INTERESTING QUESTION?

Basic income has never seriously been on the Danish agenda for practical politics, but there have been discussions on basic income since the 1970s, and most intensively and widespread at the beginning of the 1990s.

In this context, why is the debate on basic income in Denmark an interesting question?

First of all basic income is an obvious theme in a Danish context because, traditionally, Denmark conforms to the universal social democratic welfare state model characterised by relatively large universality and financed by general taxes. And basic income may be regarded as the ultimate universal welfare state model. What is the institutional logical connection between a universal social democratic model and basic income?

The institutional structure of the various welfare regimes forms the public view of the welfare client (the poor and the unemployed). Thus, the logic of universalism tends to suppress the discussion of deservingness criteria (control, need, identity, attitude and reciprocity). 'Instead of defining a line between 'them' and 'us', universal benefits and services actually help define everybody within the nation-state as belonging to one group. The vicious cycle of selective welfare policy is replaced by a positive circle' (Larsen 2007: 153). What this means is that a universal social democratic welfare regime tends to move towards a pure basic income system.

Secondly, in the last twenty years there has been a shift in Danish labour market policy where the rules for the unemployed for making themselves available to the labour market has changed from being the most liberal to being among the strictest in Europe (Goul

Andersen and Pedersen 2007). It has been called a development from welfare to workfare. How could this dramatic shift in labour market policy happen? And how should it be explained?

THE PARADIGMATIC SHIFT IN THE DANISH LABOUR MARKET AND SOCIAL POLICY

The Danish labour market and social policy in the 1970s and in the beginning of the '80s had a strong emphasis on social rights and social security. To a great extent the Danish welfare state reflected the ideals and principles of equal democratic citizenship in the sense of Marshall (Loftager 1996).

The unemployment benefit system, as it was organised up to 1994/95, showed significant similarities to a basic income system (Christensen and Loftager 2000: 258). Firstly, it was easy to get access to it. Secondly, the period of support was rather long. Thirdly, because of the high level of unemployment, the obligation to being available to the labour market was rather formal. Fourthly, there was a steady increase in the number of people taking out insurances. Therefore, it would seem as if Denmark in the beginning of the 1990s was developing along a 'basic income path'. Part of the labour market and social reform in 1993/94 pointed in that direction. A 'transitional allowance' for the long term unemployed was extended to the 50-54 years old. Parental and educational leaves were improved, and a new sabbatical leave (the one most resembling basic income) was introduced.

On the other hand, the active labour market policy reform in 1993/94 also introduced a new activation path. The period of receiving unemployment allowances was reduced to 7 years, and from that time on it was not possible to regain entitlement through activation, and a right and duty to activation for the unemployed and the social client was introduced. Throughout the 1990s the activation path was adjusted with more emphasis on motivation and economic incentives to work, stronger criteria of conditionality and shorter duration of benefits.

This policy change was already prepared by a change in economic paradigms and elite discourses (Goul Andersen and Larsen 2008). In 1988/89 a new interpretation of unemployment – as 'structural unemployment' – first appeared in government papers. It was a part of an international movement with the view that the high level of unemployment was not a matter of insufficient demand for labour power but of structural problems in the labour market. It created the frame and the diagnostic background for using the new instruments of the activation policy. Simultaneously, the unemployment rate dropped, and one of the elements in the basic income path, the leave arrangement, was phased out. As Peter Hall (1993) has shown in the British context, 'ideas matter', and in Denmark the new economic idea about structural unemployment got a foothold among experts and politicians and exerted an effect on policy change along the activation path in the 1990s.

BASIC INCOME AS A HERETICAL DISCOURSE

The first article tells the story of the ups and downs of the basic income question in Denmark. The debate on basic income started in Denmark with the book *Oprør fra midten* (Meyer et. al.1978), *Revolt from the Centre* (Meyer et. al. 1982) which triggered a broad public debate in Denmark and sold more than 100,000 copies in Denmark (a country with five million inhabitants).

In the 1980s, attempts were made to turn the idea into a political issue, in other words, to establish a political discourse about basic income. It followed that the idea had to be linked to the solution of a series of specific problems, and that efforts had to be made to form a coalition or political alliance around the issue. But the initiatives, which attempted to put it on the agenda in the 1980s, failed in the first instance.

In the beginning of the 1990s, the time for bringing the basis income question on the political agenda had come. The unemployment rate was high, and, as previously mentioned, the labour market and social system had elements of a basic income path which could be developed into a pure basic income system.

The labour market reform in 1993/94, which supported both a basic income path and a new activation path, opened a battle between the two lines and discourses. The active line was supported by the political elites and their new economic ideas of structural unemployment, while the basic income issue was brought back on the agenda by new political networks and minority groups in various political parties due to the unemployment crisis (10-12%) which had made the majority of the population lose faith in the ideology of full employment.

From 1995, the unemployment rate dropped and a new labour market policy was implemented; basic income was excluded from the public debate and from the political parties and came to be considered a heretical political discourse by the new hegemonic workfare discourse which made it a target of negative political stereotyping.

Basic income and workfare

The subject of the second article is the paradigm shift in the labour market and social policy in Denmark in the 1990s marked by the introduction of a completely new interpretation of rights and obligations in the welfare system: the right to social transfers was linked to a work obligation.

There is considerable disagreement among Danish social scientists about the interpretation of the development in the new labour market and social policy. In order to give a broad picture of the debate on activation among Danish social scientists, I present both sides in the debate, those who support it and regard it as a form of empowerment, and those who are more critical to it and see it as a disciplinary instrument.

In the article I argue that the new labour market policy is in fact workfare, a disciplinary device of work for welfare that erodes the social rights of the unemployed. In the context of the history of labour movement, it shows how the meaning of rights and obligations has changed dramatically.

The early labour movement was fighting for new rights for labour. Later on the strategy was changed to a right to labour, while the new workfare strategy meant an obligation to labour.

This signifies that the Danish Social Democratic Party's interpretation of rights and obligations within a workfare paradigm not only breaks with the original ideological foundation which meant equal political rights and responsibilities and protection of wage work, but also with the core meaning of the welfare state after the Second World War. The original idea behind the welfare state was that, with respect to the relation between rights and responsibilities, everyone had a right to work, and the state had an obligation to secure full employment. The goal of full employment was connected with the Constitution's self-provision obligation. Another element was the right to universal social transfers made possible by universal tax liability.

The new workfare policy with the slogan 'no rights without responsibilities' consists in compulsory activation of the poor. In contrast, the basic income paradigm brings new concepts of rights and responsibilities based on a universal right to a minimum income as compensation for the unpaid, socially necessary work of all citizens, corresponding to a joint universal tax liability.

BASIC INCOME AND FEMINISM

The third article discusses the background for the modest feminist interest in basic income in Denmark. Most feminists have had more focus on increasing women's participation on the labour market (commodification) than on securing economic independence in relation to the labour market (decommodification). Why?

One reason for this is that the women's movement has been locked into a *Wollstonecraft's dilemma* between equality and difference. However, a universal basic income may fulfil both the desire for equality and for diversity, as argued by the American philosopher Nancy Fraser who has redefined the gender political dilemmas in the welfare state.

There are signs that the women's movement and feminist scholars are changing their view on the normative function of wage work, but basic income is still provocative to many feminists.

WELFARE DISCOURSES AND BASIC INCOME

In the fourth article, I compare the diagnoses and solutions of the main problems in the Danish welfare state within three different social disciplines (law, economics, political science) in order to reach a deeper understanding of why interdisciplinary discussions are a rare phenomenon, and how scientific paradigms may be used to legitimate the hegemonic workfare discourse.

The paradigm shift in the Danish welfare state looks very different in the eyes of three leading social scientists in the public debate (from the legal, economic and political world respectively), though all declare their support to the Danish model and the hegemonic discourse. However, they differ in their understanding of the model and in the stories they tell about it.

In the legal perspective, the focus is on the change of the welfare model from a 'taxpayer concept' to something which is more like an 'insurance concept'. The economist wants a more profound paradigm shift by establishing a clear link between contribution and cost. Finally, the political scientist is focused on steering and consensus problems and does not see workfare as a break with the universal character of the welfare model.

In 2003, the Danish government formed a Welfare Commission with the defined task of carrying out an analysis of the expected development and of the current possibilities for reforming the welfare system. The commission consisted mainly of economists, while sociologists, political scientists and social workers, who had been engaged in the welfare policy, were not represented. In this way the commission ensured a hegemonic economic discourse.

The dominance of the economic perspective has as one of its consequences that the perspectives of the legal, sociological and political sciences are suppressed in the political-administrative debate. And even today many political scientists adapt to the economists' supremacy, and they have but few visions for the development of the citizenship. Like the economists, they function as tools for the political rulers, just in their own manner. Technically, they provide the politicians with models and arguments for making 'reforms' (e.g. cuts in the existing universal model).

The citizenship perspective, in particular, suffers from this suppression. If a basic income perspective is to win more support in the future, both in the academic world and in the public opinion, a change in the general political neoliberal climate must take place. A significant step would be if the economists' expert monopoly could be broken in relation to the work in public commissions. It would require that politicians, to a much greater extent, would start using other social scientists for advice, and that they would stimulate a much more pluralistic democratic debate among scientists, the general public and the politicians.

A GLOBAL ECOLOGICAL ARGUMENT FOR A BASIC INCOME

The subject of the last article is on what an ecological argument for a basic income would look like.

The American economist Herman E. Daly has created a paradigm for a *steady state economy*. According to Daly, there is a connection between sustainability and social justice leading to a form of basic income. Daly's argument for a basic income must, however, be extended. Daly does not point to any direct connection between basic income and the ecological limits. The ecological limits are secured by a physical system of quotas which is fixed politically and managed by companies.

The material link between the ecological limits and basic income is the so-called *ecological footprint* which is an estimate of the amount of biologically productive land and sea area needed to regenerate (if possible) the resources a human population consumes and to absorb and render harmless the corresponding waste, given prevailing technology and current knowledge.

The implementation of a global basic income would have to include a global eco-tax on the ecological footprint as part of its financial basis. The overconsumption of the rich countries appears as a large ecological footprint, and the underconsumption of the poor countries appears as poverty, a small ecological footprint. A basic income in the poor part of the world may be part of a solution to the poverty problems, while an eco-tax together with a basic income in the rich part of the world may be an element in a solution to the pollution and overconsumption problems.

Another way of conceiving a global basic income is in the form of a dividend with the premise that we all have an equal property right to the earth. When the world's citizens lend their right to nature (quota) to companies and states, they receive an income. In practice, this sale with quotas may be carried out by independent funds (like pension funds) to secure all an equal cash payment of the dividend.

BASIC INCOME BETWEEN EXCLUSION AND INCLUSION

In the closing article I discuss how to achieve a basic income. What political strategy should be followed?

Today, basic income is not on the dominating political agenda; it is excluded. The hegemonic workfare discourse is maintained by making the public view and define the basic income counter-discourse as being either entirely within (included) or entirely outside the system (excluded), and by letting the opposing forces be captured by this imagery and behave as if they were in fact inside or outside.

The ideal for a social movement wanting to change the system is to be placed in a position where it is neither included nor excluded. In such a position it is part of the political agenda without being seized by the dominating trend. It has connections and alliances with actors in the system while also contradicting it on crucial points. This is the message from the Norwegian sociologist of law Thomas Mathiesen (1982) who used the concept 'the unfinished' of a discourse that would function as an alternative to the inclusion and the exclusion process of the hegemonic discourse. 'The unfinished' is characterised by being both in opposition and in a competitive relation to the existing system. By being placed in a position both inside and outside of the system, the movement has a chance of moving the system while it is powerless when it is either included or excluded.

Basic income is fascinating as a subject because, on the whole, it moves away from this dualistic perception. It is linked to a number of practical problems and to great reforms. It represents a continuation of elements in the existing system and a discontinuation of other tendencies. It is concerned with short term questions while also having long term perspectives. It concurs with certain elements of the existing welfare system and not with others.

In other words, basic income must, to be able to transcend the dualistic view, be both 'realistic' and 'utopian' in the sense that it must show how it could be implemented within a realistic time horizon and with realistic costs, while also being an expression of a new conception of justice which may do away with the injustice that is part of the existing system.

THE DANISH BASIC INCOME MOVEMENT

The *Danish Basic Income Movement* ('Borgerlønsbevægelsen', www.borgerloen.dk) was founded in January 2000 at the initiative of members of various political parties (socialist, liberal and green) and some non-party political engaged persons with the purpose of promoting the idea of a basic income in the public opinion and among the political parties.

The supporters of basic income have very different long-term goals. To some of them, basic income is part of the process of establishing a form of socialism, to others, it is a next step towards a humanistic society, or a social democratic welfare state, and to yet others, it is an instrument in the creation of a new liberal welfare society.

The explicit objective for this cross-party movement is to put the idea of an unconditional basic income on the political agenda in Denmark. The movement has organised meetings and seminars and has initiated the publication of new books about basic income: (Engelbreth Larsen 2002), (Christensen 2004C) and (Christensen et al. 2007).

Citizen's Income as a Heretical Political Discourse: the Danish Debate about Citizen's Income

Introduction

The idea that everyone should be guaranteed a minimum income has a long history. The Catalan thinker Joan Luis Vives (1492-1540) and the English revolutionary Thomas Paine (1737-1809) were pioneers in formulating ways of providing a guaranteed income for all citizens.

In the period after World War II the idea of a citizen's income has come to be associated especially with the English liberal economist and politician, Lady Juliet Rhys-Williams (Rhys-Williams 1943), who in 1942 proposed a 'social dividend' as a counterpart to the Beveridge plan. Whereas Beveridge's prime concerns were with employment and retirement, Rhys-Williams set out a scheme to provide everybody with a social dividend.

Internationally, there seems to be much conceptual confusion around the notion of a citizen's income. A multiplicity of different terms are used in English: 'negative income tax', 'basic income', 'state bonus', 'social credit', 'social wage', 'social dividend', 'guaranteed income', 'universal benefit', 'citizen's wage' or 'citizen's income'. In the end, 'basic income' was agreed upon in 1992 when the cross-national European association for research on the subject decided to adopt a single common term.

In Danish, too, the labels vary: citizen's wage, social wage, guaranteed minimum income, social income; and ideas of this sort spread quite widely in Denmark after the publication of the book, *Oprør fra midten* (Meyer et. al.1978), *Revolt from the Centre* (Meyer et. al.1982) which used the term 'citizen's wage'. In what follows, I shall use this term, in its alternative form of 'citizen's income', as it is the one that most clearly expresses the ideas involved.

The main purpose here is to present, from an international perspective, the results of an analysis of the debate in Denmark about citizen's income with a view to both redefining and further developing the ideas at issue.

The concept of a citizen's income: as an idea, as part of a scientific paradigm and as a political discourse

A citizen's income may be defined as a general right of all citizens to receive from the state sufficient support to maintain a modest material level of living, without any general obligation to make themselves available to the labour market.

This is usually regarded only as a specific policy for labour market arrangements. However, I discern four layers within the notion of a citizen's income: these concern respectively values, theory, politics and more practical or technical matters (Christensen 2000C: 76-83). The notion is then to be seen variously as an idea within a framework of conceptual understanding; as a paradigm within a framework of scientific understanding; as political discourse within a framework of political understanding; and, finally, as a set of concrete, technical measures for political and economic affairs.

Conceptually, the idea of a citizen's income reflects a particular interpretation of the relationship between the fundamental social values of sustainability, justice, freedom, equality and material security. In addition, it may be seen as an element within various social scientific paradigms concerning the allocation of resources and rights. Finally, it figures as a political discourse in the competitive contests of politics.

There are to ideas, paradigms and discourses alike features of values, theory and strategy; but these differ with respect to purpose, function and logic. Within the ideological framework, the value element is to the fore; within the paradigmatic framework, the element of theory; in political discourse, the element of strategy. There are links between the various layers of the concept and distinct social arenas. The conceptual layer of values is aligned to the arena of ideological politics, that of theory to the scientific arena, that of politics to the political arena.

It is analytically important to distinguish between the conceptual layers because the social arenas to which they correspond are different by way of function and logic. The function of ideas is to provide ideological meaning and motivation for action; that of paradigms, to create new knowledge and understanding; that of political discourses, to bring about political understanding and support from political actors for certain political solutions, to the exclusion of other and undesired solutions. There are to a degree, nonetheless, value-related determining influences from one layer to another. Specific interpretations of the relationship between freedom, equality and justice will, for example, set the shape of the various scientific theories and paradigms that bear on resource distribution. Social scientific paradigms in turn play a part in determining the problem-specifications of political discourse. Finally, considerations of political strategy may set the course for or against concrete policy proposals.

The Danish debate of the 1990s around the subject showed that the political discourses both for and against a citizen's income drew on scientific paradigms. The hegemonic growth-discourse thus sought support from the interpretations dominant in economic science in order to exclude the opposing citizen's income discourse from the agenda. Adherents of the latter discourse, by contrast, drew on the work of critical social scientists influenced by new citizen's income paradigms emerging in international social science.

The distinction between different analytical layers within the concept of a citizen's income makes sense and helps towards clarity because the past twenty years' debate in Denmark around the idea has moved unevenly and has been conducted on different stages, and with different actors, in three periods as follows.

1. The late 1970s and early 1980s saw the launch of notions of a citizen's income by 'outsiders' in various ideological environments. This meant that the debate then stayed mainly at the layer of values and theory.
2. In the course of the 1980s, a new social movement, Midteroprøret (the Centre Revolt), arose which, inspired by the book *Oprør fra midten* (Meyer et al. 1978 and 1982), turned the issue of a citizen's income into a new political discourse through its attempts to place the question on the political agenda. In the same period, the idea cropped up in the scientific arena, both internationally and in Denmark, to become a feature of a number of new social scientific paradigms.
3. New formulations of citizen's income as political discourse were brought to bear in the early 1990s. Debate about the notion now spread among the public at large as an item on the general political agenda concerning renewal of the welfare state. That debate was set going both 'from the bottom up' by initiatives from new political networks and 'from the top down' by initiatives from various reporting commissions, research workers and politicians.

THE EMERGENCE OF A NEW IDEA OF CITIZEN'S INCOME IN THE 1970S

The interesting feature of the climate of ideological debate in the 1970s is that, in relative independence of one another, 'outsiders' in four different ideological settings – social-democratic, socio-liberal,

Marxist and liberal – advanced parallel notions of introducing new social provision for maintenance of livelihood without traditional wage labour in return (Christensen 2000C: 216-263).

1. The Swedish economist, Gunnar Adler-Karlsson, then a professor at Roskilde University Centre in Denmark, published a couple of books in the mid-1970s (Adler-Karlsson, 1976 and 1977) which put a social-democratic case for a 'guaranteed minimum income'.
2. The idea of a citizen's income aroused widespread public attention in Denmark, especially through publication of the book *Oprør fra midten* by the philosopher Villy Sørensen, the natural scientist Niels I. Meyer and the politician Kristen Helveg Petersen, in February 1978. This linked the idea to socio-liberal circles and to new 'green' aspirations for 'a humanely balanced society'.
3. At around the same time the ideas of the Austrian/French socialist André Gorz about introduction of a 'social income' came to be known, in socialist circles in particular, through translation of several of his books (Gorz 1979, 1981 and 1983).
4. Finally, a former cooperative society director, Niels Hoff, launched the notion of a 'citizen's stipend' for debate in liberal circles (Hoff 1983).

These very diverse authors were at one and the same time each linked to a particular ideological milieu while yet having an outsider status in relation to it. They figured as typical heretics, conceptual innovators and provocateurs who 'stood things on their head', broke away from established ideological frameworks and challenged industrial society's conventional growth discourse.

Common to the four strands of thought was an assured awareness that the familiar measures to solve societal problems were inadequate and that prevailing conceptions of nature and humankind in industrial society were wide open to question. With these authors' shifts of conceptual framework went also shifts in the language and the metaphors they used. New views of problems and solutions will usually find reflection in language. For in the designation of one thing as a problem and another as a solution, problems are often described negatively, solutions positively. If things are switched around, new words are commonly needed to reflect the new insights.

So there was turbulence in four separate ideological settings; and, if hesitantly and tentatively, a movement emerged towards formulation of a new common ideology, towards a sustainable development that was to include within it the notion of a citizen's income in some form or other. To borrow a term from the philosopher of science Thomas Kuhn (Kuhn 1962), the situation was pre-paradigmatic. But though there were many similarities of approach between the four currents of thinking, there were nonetheless also significant differences; and no dialogue between them came about.

A NEW GRASSROOTS MOVEMENT AND ITS FORMATION OF A POLITICAL DISCOURSE ON CITIZEN'S INCOME IN THE 1980s

The thoughts of Adler-Karlsson, Gorz and Hoff came to be known only within small circles and were quickly forgotten. It was *Oprør fra midten* and its conception of a citizen's income that stirred public debate.

Publication of this book led to the establishment of a new periodical, the formation of a new grassroots movement and publication of a series of further books. A network was set up which served as a political agent to disseminate the new ideas. It came as a surprise to the initiators that the notion of a citizen's income proved to be among those ideas that attracted greatest immediate support. It was this notion, therefore, which the new grassroots movement took up first with a view to translation into concrete policy (Christensen 2000C: 264-284).

So an attempt was made in the 1980s to turn the idea into a 'political issue', to set in motion a political discourse about citizen's incomes. It followed that the idea had to be linked to solution of a series of specific political problems, and that efforts must be made to form a coalition or political alliance around the issue. The means adopted to this end were a number of conferences, publication of discussion books and pamphlets, interviews with leading politicians. The prime objective was to build a political alliance around the issue between the trade union movement, the Social Democratic Party (Socialdemokratiet), the Social Liberal Party (Det Radikale Venstre) and the Socialist People's Party (Socialistisk Folkeparti).

The new grassroots movement had to engage actively in the game of practical politics and show that it was not just preoccupied with utopian ideas, in order to get into debate and dialogue with the political parties and the union movement. It therefore put forward an alternative national budget and made specific proposals to provide a citizen's income for young people and for others to have access to 'sabbatical leave'. The movement for 'revolt from the centre' failed in its endeavours to recruit the old political parties that were its target for its policies of citizen's incomes, or to persuade them to incorporate similar proposals in their programmes. Yet, although its hopes of thus putting the issue directly onto the everyday political agenda failed in the first instance, its ideas about general provision for state-supported sabbatical leave were to prove significant for the subsequent acceptance of schemes of this sort in the late 1980s and early 1990s.

It must be said, then, that the political counter-discourse initiated in the 1980s only took a weak form.

Its weakness of strategy was that its proponents failed to link the idea, with sufficient clarity and certainty, to a wider range of concrete social problems. It was not made clear that citizen's incomes imply a strategy towards a multiplicity of goals. There was a failure to specify the relevance of the idea to resolution of the problems confronting the unemployed, social assistance recipients, people on early retirement, disability pensioners and so on, in respect of their circumstances of dependency as against their claims to personal autonomy. There was also in the 1980s, moreover, an unfortunate tendency to division of the debate around citizen's incomes into two parts, one ideological and the other more practical, with the result that the new and weak political discourse came quickly to figure in a form bereft of conceptual elaboration and coherence.

The idea of a citizen's income had now taken material root in a social movement which sought to place the issue on the political agenda. But this also meant that the movement for 'revolt from the centre' had acquired a 'monopoly' on the issue which in turn prevented the formation of a cross-political forum between social democrats, 'greens', liberals and Marxists to take the matter further.

CITIZEN'S INCOME AS A POLITICAL DISCOURSE IN THE ARENA OF POLITICS IN THE 1990s

In the early 1990s – especially in the years 1992-94 – the citizen's income debate reappeared in different guise. A new discourse on the theme was created in the form of a counter-discourse to the dominant discourse around the labour market and social policy concerning renewal of the welfare state (Christensen 2000C: 285-459).

The idea of a citizen's income took on new shape as a political discourse because the movement-oriented, the scientific and the political strands of debate about the issue came, for a short time, to be twined together. A number of parties took up the question. New cross-political fora were created, and the idea became a subject of social scientific analysis. For a brief period the new citizen's income discourse thus managed to give voice to sentiments widespread among the population and to sow the seeds of a new pattern of alliance between groups across a series of political divides.

The interesting feature of the 1990s' debate about the issue was that the idea of a citizen's income was brought on the political agenda, both 'from the bottom upwards' and 'from the top downwards'. It came 'from the bottom upwards' in the sense that it was promoted by marginalised people themselves, by 'outsiders' on the fringes of the world of business and trade unions, by spinners of ideas and by a few practitioners and controversialists of social science; and a new journal, SALT, strove to join the debates in the party-political arena with the debates in the arenas of social science and social movements. 'From the top downwards', in turn, the new discourse was met by attempts to limit, diminish or exclude it: attempts to those ends were made by the leadership of the established political parties, by a number of ministers, and by public commissions of enquiry and civil servants.

The fact that the issue of citizen's income got on the official agenda of politics in the years 1992-94 can be ascribed to the development of a particular political context and its coincidence with a set of economic, institutional and political circumstances.

The problems of unemployment and transfer payments were attracting growing attention since joblessness continued to rise until the turn of the year 1994-95. At the beginning of the 1990s the government had set up a series of commissions of enquiry whose tasks were to devise a more rational system of labour market arrangements and public benefit provision: the targets were simplification and savings. In 1993, moreover, the new social-democratic government had enacted a set of measures for reform of the labour market. On the one hand, these widened employees' opportunities to take periods of paid leave away from work; on the other hand, they gave significantly more scope for 'activation', that is to say enforcement on the jobless of obligations to enter training schemes or find work.

By 1992-93 the hegemonic growth-discourse was in crisis over its legitimacy in popular eyes. The majority of the population had lost faith in the ideology of full employment. Public opinion polls showed widespread attitudes in favour of rethinking labour market policies and experimenting with alternative models for distribution: 'dustmen's deal' models, for instance, along the lines for job-sharing proposed by the dustmen in Aarhus; or measures for reduced working-time, or for a citizen's income. In that situation, the latter notion indeed came to figure as a serious alternative. Politicians and their parties were forced into taking some stance on the idea of citizen's income, and to spell out arguments against such new and more radical modes of problem solving.

The fact that the discourse for a citizen's income vanished again from the official political arena around the turn of the year 1994/95 must be attributed to a change in the conjunctures of economics and politics, and to associated success for the hegemonic growth discourse in its endeavours to exclude the rival discourse. That exclusion of the citizen's income discourse took place, at a rhetorical level, in public political debate and within the political parties; and this was matched, at an institutional level, by exclusion of discourse about job sharing, sabbatical leave provision and citizen's income from the work of the Social Commission, the Welfare Commission and the government's Economic Secretariat. It is the task of a hegemonic discourse to set the official definitions of what are to be recognised as problems, and of how those problems fit in with existing institutions. The aim is to maintain a viable common identity and a political coalition. This is often done by way of public commissions of enquiry and civil service reports; and the concrete means to the end are the terms of reference set for commission enquiry, the appointments made to commissions, and the formulation of their professional and technical discourse.

The fact that it proved hard for the idea of a citizen's income to make headway within the political parties is connected with the point that, to a greater or lesser extent, most of the parties were coloured by and linked into the ideologies and organisational forms of established industrial society, whose hegemonic discourse was challenged by the discourse for a citizen's income. Those parties most clearly committed to the goal of economic growth were also the parties most strongly opposed to the idea of a citizen's income; while parties semi-critical of growth – such as the Socialist People's Party (Socialistisk Folkeparti) and the Social Liberal Party (Det Radikale Venstre) – held views on the idea that were ambivalent and unclear. The Social Democrats (Socialdemokratiet) and the right-of-centre, Denmark's Liberal Party (Venstre) now found themselves with a new enemy in common, under the name of citizen's income, against whom they were in agreement to keep the societal goal of economic growth intact and to step up compulsory 'activation' for work and job-training. Both these parties then amended their programmes to distance themselves from the idea of a citizen's income.

The failure of the citizen's income discourse to gain a foothold was tied up also with the fact that it achieved little support from circles central in social critique of the time. To these the notion either seemed too controversial and so was ignored, or it was ridiculed as unrealistic. The leading spirits of the women's movement thus dismissed the idea without explicitly addressing it. And the left-wing think-tank CASA (Centre for Alternative Social Analysis), which served as an expert body for the left in trade union and political affairs, opposed the hegemonic discourse for economic growth, yet held back from taking any stance on the idea of a citizen's income. CASA instead looked to an enlargement of wage-earning work as the way forward, to be achieved through job-sharing and the creation of new 'green' jobs in the public sector. An independent cross-political debating group similarly distanced itself from the citizen's income discourse and proposed that wage-employment be expanded by means of new jobs in the private service sector. Taken together, these responses demonstrated the continuing hold of the ideology of wage labour over even the critical flank of public commentary.

CITIZEN'S INCOME AS A METAPHOR IN VARIOUS FRAMEWORK-NARRATIVES

For the purpose of my analysis I see conceptions of a citizen's income as an interesting new societal metaphor (Christensen 2000C: 50-60, 354-357, 446-448).

A metaphor is an expression used to describe one thing by referring to another with similar qualities, usually in an imaginative way which offers a new perspective on the world. Metaphors can be used as epistemological tools for conceptual and scientific analysis towards the creation of new ideas and approaches. Concepts and scientific models derive from some basic metaphors, and scientific innovations often take the form of a shift of metaphors. Metaphors are organised into hierarchical structures of meaning or frameworks of understanding. All theories of society may therefore be seen as metaphorical systems based upon some foundational metaphors or 'metaphors in depth'.

For all citizen's income theorists, development of the concept involves endeavours to establish a new language, including new metaphors distinct from those of the dominant scientific paradigms and political discourses. To talk about a citizen's income or wage, is an attempt to give a name to a new situation by creating a new concept through a combination of old concepts. A 'wage' is an economic concept that has something to do with markets, whereas the concept of 'citizen' has something to do with state, society and democracy. The new concept of a 'citizen's wage' implies a proposal to add to the market wage another wage that is politically determined. This in turn means giving democracy a more prominent part in distribution and so implies a new priority for the role of fellow-citizenship vis à vis the role of markets.

Public welfare payments are usually seen as providing a 'safety net'. Some critics of the welfare state argue, however, that many such benefits have become rather a 'hammock' that encourages idleness. So instead, they discuss how to turn welfare provision into a 'springboard' for work enterprise. All these phrases are examples of the widespread use of metaphors.

So too with the notion of a citizen's income which is to be, not a benefit payment contingent on restrictively defined need or past contribution, but a universal personal entitlement. It thus shatters the familiar one-sided view of transfer incomes. The aims of a citizen's income are multiple; and just which aims are to prevail will be a matter for individual recipients to decide. So citizen's income may be seen as both a 'safety net' and a 'springboard'; and yet it can be used as a 'hammock' too. People also have a need to rest and to decide just how and when for themselves.

A number of current transfer payments and arrangements in support of enterprise can be replaced by, and reconceived as, a universal citizen's income. When such reconceptions are followed through, an entirely different understanding emerges, a new vision. The new metaphor of a citizen's income thus helps to change society's economic-cum-political conception of normality. Everyone will be normal and equal by way of common entitlement to an assured citizen's income. The old concepts are left behind – transfer payments, welfare benefits, social assistance, leave of absence, compensation and so on, all of which in some way or other incorporate the notion of wage labour as the norm. A citizen's income will not abolish wage labour; but it will relativise it, by depriving it of its monopoly on normality and so of its hegemonic role.

Citizen's income figures as a new metaphor within frameworks of understanding which conceive society as primarily a commonalty, a democracy or a civil society, for which the market metaphor has only secondary significance. So, as a new metaphor, that of citizen's income points to a new scale of priorities among the various societal metaphors applied to current welfare society. A society of citizen's income is one that is understood to be, first and foremost, not a labour market but rather a democracy so set as to ensure autonomy and security of living vis à vis the labour market and the state within a civil society. Provision for a citizen's income will not have the power to dissolve the market character of society or its features of political compulsion. But it will set some clearer limits to that character and those features; and arrayed against this vision are most of those sceptics or opponents of the idea of citizen's income who, consciously or unconsciously, see society primarily as a market and the market metaphor as basic.

Frameworks of understanding are systems of metaphors. Coherence within a framework of understanding is created out of narratives, and it is through narratives that metaphors and the pattern they form become visible. The metaphor of citizen's income can be located within four different frame-setting narratives.

At the most general level the idea of citizen's income may be understood by reference to a narrative about the crises of ideologies and industrialism and about the limits to growth in which citizen's income figures as part of a new narrative concerning sustainable development (Christensen 2000C: 204-208). The seeds of this new narrative were planted by the citizen's income theorists of the 1970s and acquired scientific form in the work of, in particular, the ecologically oriented economist Herman E. Daly (Daly 1977).

Next, the idea of citizen's income may be set within the story of the historical development of democracy and the welfare state where it appears as a further stage of welfare provision and a full realisation of social citizenship: the formation of some sort of 'third way society' where the aspiration is to unite old and new political forces in a new manner.

Within those parameters in turn, citizen's income may be viewed more narrowly by reference to a smaller narrative about the problems of the welfare state and about endeavours towards greater autonomy for the citizen vis à vis state, market and civil society alike.

Finally, the idea of a citizen's income may be seen as a feature of some more technical narratives about simplification and rationalisation of a series of welfare-societal mechanisms.

CITIZEN'S INCOME AS METONYMY AND A TARGET OF NEGATIVE POLITICAL STEREOTYPING

In the early 1990s the citizen's income debate took the form of an ideological contest over the norms implied by linguistic usage. Supporters of the idea fought for acknowledgement of the concept of citizen's income as a new term with a core meaning that was neutral, and a complementary meaning that was positive. Opponents sought instead to accord to the term both core and complementary meanings of a negative character (Christensen 2000C: 59-60, 414-416, 457-458).

While supporters used the concept as metaphor, opponents used it as metonymy to the effect of negative political stereotyping. Whereas metaphors are aimed to create new meanings by conjoining two different contexts, metonymy involves the making of links only between features that conventionally belong to one and the same context. Thus opponents of the citizen's income idea strove to associate it with a range of adverse features of the established system. They described provision for it as provision for 'enforced passivity', as something that would 'set no challenges', as 'morally demeaning'. They argued that some particular negative features of current welfare provision would be writ large in any institution of citizen's income. And from this they drew general inferences about the nature of a new entity, the citizen's income society, which they then stamped as undesirable.

Metaphorical use of the concept of citizen's income aims to open people's eyes to an alternative social order involving a new enhancement of the rights of fellow-citizenship and a sustainable development of civil society. Metonymic use of the concept, by contrast, has been deployed to strengthen the foundations of the established order.

CITIZEN'S INCOME AS A POINTER TO A SHIFT OF IDEAS, PARADIGMS AND PROBLEM RESOLUTIONS

Another theoretical perspective on the idea of a citizen's income is to see it as a sign of a shift of values at the normative level and a shift of paradigms at the scientific level (Christensen 2000C: 207-208).

At the normative level, the shift involved is from values that emphasise economic growth and equality (distributive justice) to values that emphasise freedom (autonomy), justice and sustainability. At the scientific level, the concept of a citizen's income may be seen as an element in a set of new social-scientific paradigms which stand in opposition to the paradigms prevailing in that field of knowledge.

Political ideologies and scientific theories alike may be described as larger coherent systems for problem resolution, within which there are internal connections of common logic among the descriptions and explanations offered of the various problems and problem-solutions. What is characteristic of a paradigm shift is that problems and solutions are turned upside down by changes in viewpoints, values and language. Previous conceptions of what constitutes a problem are radically reformulated. The problem itself takes on a new character and shape. Problems change places with solutions, in the sense that they come to be seen as parts of the solution, while what previously figured as solutions come now to be seen as part of the problem.

The ideological outsiders who brought the notion of a citizen's income to Denmark in the late 1970s and early 1980s – Adler-Karlsson and Gorz in particular – spearheaded a shift of ideas and paradigms. What this involved was – to borrow a term from the American sociologist, Alvin W. Gouldner (Gouldner 1971) – a distinct change of 'domain assumptions', with common agreement to abandon a hitherto dominant economic conception of humankind and to pursue a new awareness of the limits to human exploitation of nature. With this went also a common concern to diagnose social systems that had got into crisis over their modes of problem solution to such a point that 'vicious circles' had set in.

The 1980s gave birth to the idea of citizen's income as an element of new paradigms in international social science. There were five of these – 1. an ecologically oriented economic paradigm (Herman E. Daly 1990); 2. a paradigm of procedural law (Jürgen Habermas 1996); 3. a paradigm of citizenship (Bill Jordan 1992 and Claus Offe 1992); 4. a feminist paradigm (Nancy Fraser 1994); and 5. a liberal property-paradigm (Samuel Brittan 1995). All of them differed radically from the paradigms of the market and public choice hitherto dominant in social science; and it is on this score that the idea of a citizen's income can be seen as generating a paradigmatic shift.

Despite their diversity of theoretical perspectives, language and traditions, these five new paradigms all have a significant feature in common: they see provision of a citizen's income as a way towards a fairer society and as a breach with traditional conceptions of equality. They also all set their faces against a conventional market-economic understanding of society; and they join the idea of citizen's income to an argument that the state has a special part to play, an active role superordinate to that of the market, in creating justice in society.

The emergence and development of the notion of citizen's income, in a variety of separate versions during the 1970s and '80s, can be construed as a shift of ideas and paradigms in relation to the prevailing modes of conceptual and social-scientific understanding. Yet no new common system of ideas, no new single and coherent counter-paradigm to set against that of the economic market, came to fruition in consequence. There was only the germ of a new idea and of a new paradigm about sustainable development.

Citizen's income as a case of 'the unfinished'

My analysis of the Danish debate about citizen's income draws on a range of concepts and an approach developed by the Norwegian sociologist of law, Thomas Mathiesen (Mathiesen 1982 and 1992). He has explored the way in which a hegemonic discourse is created by means, on the one hand, of marginalising (excluding) alternative discourses and, on the other hand, of socialising (including) potential alliance-opponents within a mode of perception common to the political public. Inclusion means that efforts are made to absorb opponents into the hegemonic alliance by presenting the common features of deviant action as disadvantageous. Exclusion means that opponents are expelled through presentation of their action as wrong-headed (Christensen 2000C: 89-92, 477-80).

Mathiesen lists a series of rhetorical techniques for inclusion directed to erasing disagreement with the hegemonic discourse. The aim is to render potential opponents powerless by presenting them as being in essential agreement with that discourse. But he notes also a series of rhetorical techniques for exclusion which by contrast underline the disagreement with the hegemonic discourse and characterise it as fundamental. This technique involves labelling the disagreement as Utopian, abstract and dangerous. The aim here is to render opponents powerless by presenting them as being in basic conflict with the system.

The hegemonic discourse is thus maintained by persuading the public at large to perceive and define counter-discourses as being either wholly within or wholly outside the system; and by encouraging opponents themselves to be captured by this imagery, to the point of actually behaving as if they indeed were either within the system or outside it. To establish counter-power, it is therefore essential to avoid being captured by the imagery of the dominant discourse; and this in turn means demonstrating, in a variety of theoretical and practical ways, that the logic of 'either-or' is spurious and needs to be replaced by a logic of 'both-and'.

The alternative to 'inclusion' and 'exclusion' alike is what Mathiesen calls 'the unfinished'. This involves adopting a stance that is both opposed to the established system and in competition with it. Mathiesen uses the term 'competing contradiction' to describe such a relationship, and he calls it 'unfinished' because it offers only a sketch, an outlined prospect towards solutions, not a definitive answer or a final solution. It is unfinished or incomplete in the sense that it has not been tested and that its consequences remain uncertain. The risk to which 'the unfinished' is exposed is either that it may be made 'complete' through incorporation within the system as just a small positive reform; or that it may be wholly excluded from the system as a remote and utopian fantasy.

The idea of citizen's income can be taken as an example of an 'unfinished' idea which has maintained recurrent vitality just because it has served as a mode of 'competing contradiction' vis à vis current welfare society. But the history of this idea has been marked at the same time by tendencies towards both inclusion and exclusion. In the debate on the issue during the 1990s, opponents tended to depict suggestions for a citizen's income as the adoption of an irresponsible line of policy, advocated by theorists remote from real life and hostile to practical short-term measures for improvement. These are typical rhetorical tactics for exclusion.

In fact, proponents of a citizen's income have always been faced with a dilemma whether to emphasise the proposition as an idea within a wider context, or to put it forward as merely a technical measure. Technical sketches towards practical implementation of citizen's income have in some circumstances helped to give the idea appeal by way of 'competing contradiction'. That was the case, to some degree, in the 1980s and early 1990s. But there is then a large risk that ideas are quickly downgraded to matters of mere technique, and so lose meaningful coherence. It was in just this way that citizen's income advocates, in the 1980s and the 1990s alike, came to neglect the arguments that would have supported it, arguments such as a concern for the values of a democratic society. There was a shortage of actors who could bring ideas and techniques together and so give the movement that overriding dynamic which the idea of 'the unfinished' implies.

THE CITIZEN'S INCOME DEBATE AS A CONFRONTATION BETWEEN 'REACTIONARY' AND 'PROGRESSIVE' POLITICAL RHETORIC

Yet another approach to analysis of the issue is to see politics as a contest between diverse political discourses in which processes of hegemony formation and exclusion take place. Political discourses arise out of the political process and have both a rhetorical and an institutional aspect to them (Christensen 2000C: 85-87, 452-457).

The American social scientist Albert O. Hirschman (Hirschman 1991) has set out some ideal-type characterisations of the patterns of argument deployed by 'reactionaries' and 'progressives' during the 200-year history of democracy. In a historical perspective it is clear that 'reactionaries' have more or less stayed with the same basic patterns of argument against liberal reformers or 'progressives': first, at the time when civil democracy was initiated by the French Revolution; second, when political democracy came about through the introduction of general suffrage; and third, when social citizenship made its way through growth of the welfare state.

From this point of view it may be said that we are now in a new phase of democratic development where the issue is how to take the welfare state further, and where the 'progressive' agenda focuses on provision for a citizen's income and sustainable development.

Hirschman identifies three typical patterns of argument against reform: 1. reforms are misguided (the 'perversity thesis') in the sense that they will have consequences other than those envisaged by reformists; 2. reforms are futile (the 'futility thesis') in the sense that they will not change things anyway; and/or 3. reforms are dangerous (the 'jeopardy thesis') in the sense that they will destroy features of the present system which are indispensable. As against these, supporters of 'progressive' reform draw on three parallel patterns of argument: 1. reforms will have a synergetic effect in a process that will lead to the solution of not just one problem but a whole complex of problems (the 'mutual support thesis'); 2. reforms are a matter of 'natural' progress or developmental 'necessity' (the thesis that 'history is on our side'); and/or 3. in the absence of reform, the system will collapse or produce a totally unacceptable state of affairs (the 'imminent-danger thesis').

The aim of both types of political rhetoric, 'reactionary' and 'progressive', is to persuade recipients of the message by reference to the various kinds of effect that will follow the implementation and, conversely, the rejection of reform. Reform opponents try to induce negative attitudes to a reform proposal by assertion that there will be no effects to reform at all, or some adverse and even dangerous effects. Reform supporters, by contrast, try to encourage positive attitudes to the proposal by claiming that it will set a virtuous circle in motion towards solution of several problems; or that it constitutes a necessity either by way of the logic of progress or in order to avoid misfortune. Both lines of argument may involve manipulation, more or less covert, unless it is made clear that neither supporters nor opponents are in fact capable of making pronouncements about future patterns of development with any certainty.

In the 1990s' debate about citizen's income, opponents resorted to the argumentation-patterns typical of 'reactionaries' in the following ways. First, introduction of a citizen's income will be misguided: as a 'passive' measure, it will create a 'group of losers', 'lead to cuts' or 'send women back to the kitchen sink'. Second, it will be useless because 'it will be futile to redefine the notion of work', 'we already have a sort of citizen's income', 'it's just another word for early retirement and disability pension'. Third, it will be dangerous: 'the unemployment funds will be transferred from trade union hands to the state', the proposal 'is in conflict with the Constitution' and/or 'will lead to economic collapse'.

Correspondingly, supporters resorted to arguments typical of the 'progressive' patterns just outlined. First, provision for a citizen's income will solve a number of linked problems: it will tackle 'problems of unemployment, environment and democracy in common context', and 'a series of social dogmas will fall like domino-pieces'. Second, it is in line with 'natural' development: it will 'round off the notion of social citizenship', it will finally 'end the subsistence logic of capitalism'. Third, it is a necessity in order to avoid danger: 'the choice is between citizen's income and barbarism'.

To a very large extent, situations in the labour market and in society at large may be seen as involving an enforced choice between 'activity' and 'passivity', between 'independence' and 'dependence', between 'wage work' and 'transfer income'. The things usually considered 'good' are activity, independence and wage work; the 'bad' things are passivity, dependence and transfer income. In the dominant dualistic universe of language, opponents of a citizen's income define provision for it in metonymic fashion as a passive transfer income that creates dependency. They adhere to the dualistic contrast between 'activity' and 'passivity', and wish to maintain this because it serves to keep work for wages in a dominant position. Citizen's income may also be construed in metaphorical fashion, however: as real freedom, as a mechanism to break up the dualisms and double-binds, and to dissolve the enforcements of choice. Seen from that angle, citizen's income reflects a shift in frameworks of understanding – a 'framing' of social conceptions – and a challenge to the linguistic and institutional dualism that prevails in society.

FURTHER DEVELOPMENT OF CITIZEN'S INCOME AS AN IDEA AND AS A PARADIGM

The idea of a citizen's income entails a change or shift in the principles by which boundaries are drawn between the different spheres of society – state, market and civil society – because it advances new principles for the distribution of money (of special interest to economists), for the distribution of rights (of special interest to political scientists), for changes in patterns of work and use of time (of special interest to sociologists) and for revision of obligations concerning work and maintenance (of special interest to lawyers).

While the citizen's income idea has often been discussed and justified by reference only to one of these spheres, whether market or state or civil society, it has been my aim to offer a cross-disciplinary and more rounded portrayal of the concept. I have tried to do so by examining six different modes of approach to interpretation of the issue, drawn from work across the social sciences internationally; and by then setting out a critical analysis of the strengths and weaknesses to be found in a range of diagnoses of the crises of the welfare state put forward by Danish social scientists. When taken together, the contributions of all these various social theorists help to sketch a fuller and more comprehensive picture of citizen's income as an idea and as a scientific paradigm. I conclude on that basis that this idea-cum-paradigm may be seen (Christensen 2000C: 508-509):

1. as a further development of democratic fellow-citizenship, more specifically as a full realisation of social citizenship
2. as an element in a process of sustainable development through its contribution to setting a political limit to the exploitation of nature
3. as a new form of property right which will make for a fairer distribution of resources in a market economy

4. as a means to creating autonomy vis à vis the market through its setting of a political limit to the commodification of labour power
5. as a means to creating autonomy also vis à vis the state through its setting of a political limit to client-dependency on the state
6. as an element in the process of creating a new gender balance

In sum, the conclusion is that citizen's income figures as a prime feature in a narrative about the further development of democratic fellow-citizenship involving a completion of social citizenship and a step towards establishment of sustainable development. Within those parameters citizen's income also figures in a range of more concrete narratives about the simultaneous creation of greater justice in the distribution of a market economy's resources (a new form of property right); and of greater freedom (autonomy) vis à vis the market (de-commodification), vis à vis the state (lessening of client dependency) and vis à vis the family and civil society (lessening of family patriarchy).

FURTHER DEVELOPMENT OF CITIZEN'S INCOME AS A FEATURE OF A NEW POLITICAL DISCOURSE ON SUSTAINABLE DEVELOPMENT

The notion of citizen's income may be seen as a feature of narratives that take the form of ideas, paradigms and political discourses alike. Seen as a paradigm the idea can be so formulated as to figure in a series of narratives that have to do with setting limits: in a narrative about setting limits to the exploitation of nature; in one which concerns setting limits to the commodification of labour power; in another which is about setting limits to client dependency on the state; and finally, in a narrative directed to setting limits to family dependency.

These narratives about limits may in turn send the ball rolling for a number of discourse-narratives about the need for a range of new social contracts. Welfare society's large social contract between labour and capital needs to be replaced by a multi-dimensional contract which will pose new limits to the exploitation of humankind and nature. This can be expressed as the need for a new version of the contract between labour and capital; and the need, simultaneously, for a set of other contracts between state and individual, between the sexes, and between generations. A new political contract for a citizen's income satisfies these requirements because arrangements for such provision will engage with them all and serve towards restoring balance as against a number of the fundamental imbalances of modern welfare society. Provision for a citizen's income will thus,

1. help to create a more equal distribution of such work as is essential for society
2. allow reinforcement of individuals' legal rights and reduce the problem of client-dependency
3. offer the basis for a fairer division of labour between the sexes
4. strengthen civil society and democracy
5. in conjunction with other measures help towards a more sustainable development

Viewed in relation to the political priorities of the various ideological frameworks of understanding, the idea of a citizen's income should in principle be capable of gaining widespread support: support from those socialists who are particularly concerned with a more equal division of societally essential labour; from those liberals who prioritise a reduction of client dependency; from those feminists to whom a fairer division of work between the sexes is a prime aim; and from those 'greens' on whose agenda a strengthening of civil society is in high place.

It is the function of political discourses to create such identity of feeling and such frameworks for action as will make for a coalition of political actors. At the beginning of the 1990s, the new discourse on citizen's income reflected some attitudes that were widespread in the population, and it helped to sow the seeds of a new pattern of political alliance across a range of well-known political divides.

A further new discourse around the idea, so pitched as to bring together support from among socialists, liberals, feminists and 'greens' on the lines sketched above, is still awaiting its realisation. History seems to show that the idea has a vitality which allows it to reappear in new shape, even after it has been forgotten for some time. My aim in this analysis has been to offer a firmer and more comprehensive basis for the next debate about citizen's income.

The Rhetoric of Rights and Obligations in Denmark from a Labour History Perspective

Introduction

In the 1990s, the Danish hegemonic discourse on welfare policy, especially in labour market and social policy, shifted from a so-called 'passive' to a so-called 'active' policy, in accordance with major international trends towards a workfare discourse.

The 1994 labour market reform, and later the 1997 Act on Active Social Policy, changed the paradigms in labour market and social policy. It represented a break with the former so-called 'passive' policy under which job and education offers qualified unemployed for continued unemployment benefits. After the labour market reform, the maximum unemployment benefit period was seven years, and activation no longer qualified for continued unemployment benefits. Before 1997, the social policy was based on an income disappearance principle. The idea was that adequate public cash benefits would prevent social stigmatisation due to loss of income, but also that the system required unemployed to be available to the regular labour market. The two reforms emphasised the universal rights and obligations for everybody to exploit and develop their skills, and restricted access to benefits. Clients who decline an activation offer are no longer entitled to social benefits. This is the background for the Social Democratic government's philosophy about rights and responsibility which dominates their new politics.

My aim in this article is to:

1. explain the shift in the political discourse from welfare to workfare in a long historical perspective. I will show how the concepts of rights and responsibilities in the ideology of the Danish labour movement have been applied in three periods of Danish labour movement history (Christensen 2000B): a) when the labour movement was a new social movement with strong reform/revolutionary ambitions: rights of labour; b) the golden age of the welfare state in the early 1970s: right to labour; and c) today, when the welfare state is changing into a workfare state: obligation to labour.
2. explain the Danish workfare discourse in different scientific analyses. Danish social scientists interpret the substance in the workfare discourse quite differently. Some are critical and others legitimise it. But how can different social scientists arrive at such disparate conceptions and evaluations of the workfare policy?
3. argue for a citizen's income reform with a new understanding of how to link rights and responsibilities. Everybody agrees that, at some basic level, all members in a society must contribute if they want to enjoy its benefits. Philosophers and social scientists therefore talk about a norm of reciprocity which exists in all societies. But the concrete interpretation of rights and responsibilities has changed. The traditional Danish welfare state had one interpretation of justice, the workfare strategy another, and a citizen's income strategy must build on yet another interpretation.

Hegemony and political discourses/scientific paradigms

Society may be seen as a hegemonic community held together by a hegemonic political discourse. This discourse reproduces and transforms society in an antagonistic interplay with other discourses (Christensen 1999 and 2000C).

In general, politics deals with the articulation of specific interests and the exclusion of rival interests. As a rule, it is only by creating alliances between actors, by establishing a hegemonic project that social power can be maintained. And a hegemonic project must be supported by a hegemonic discourse.

A scientific paradigm and a political discourse are different types of frames, which differ with respect to purpose, function and logic.

The function of a political discourse is to create political understanding and support among political actors for certain political solutions to the exclusion of other and undesired solutions.

The function of scientific paradigms is, in particular, to create new knowledge and understanding in the scientific community. This generally implies that the theoretical element (the explanatory and interpretative dimensions) is emphasised, while the normative and praxis-oriented elements are downplayed.

But often there is a connection between scientific paradigms and political discourses because social science paradigms can support and sometimes steer a political discourse.

Various conceptualisations of workfare in Danish social science

Danish social scientists conceptualise and evaluate the new activation policy in different ways: there is criticism from social workers (Carstens 1998) and social policy scientists (Abrahamson 1998), but what is most astonishing is that formerly critical neo-Marxist scientists now defend and legitimise the policy with reference to modern sociological paradigms.

One example is Jacob Torfing (1999A, 1999B), political scientist and leading theorist in the discourse theory formulated by Ernesto Laclau and Chantal Mouffe (1985) and inspired by British Marxist Bob Jessop's (1995) theory on a regime shift from a Keynesian welfare state (KWS) to a Schumpeterian workfare regime (SWR). Torfing analyses the Danish welfare state within Jessop's framework and describes the Danish workfare policy in a discourse perspective. His conclusion is that the Danish workfare strategy is 'offensive' and 'neo-statist' in contrast to UK and US policies which are described as 'defensive' and 'neo-liberal' (Torfing1999B: 5).

Another analysis of the Danish workfare system, which in some way is similar to Torfing's analysis, is sociologist Per H. Jensen's analysis (1999). He disagrees with Torfing's conceptualisations of a movement from welfare to workfare and seems to think that there has always been a sort of workfare logic in the welfare state. He sees 'activation' in a 'life politics' perspective inspired by Anthony Giddens (1994) and calls the workfare strategy 'the enabling perspective' because it enables 'the individual to achieve self-actualisation and personal autonomy' (Jensen1999: 1).

A critical perspective on the Danish workfare policy is launched by Henning Hansen, Jens Lind and Iver Hornemann Møller (2000) in a Marxist-inspired 'industrial reserve army' approach. The size and composition of the industrial reserve army may vary, but its presence is important for capital accumulation since its function is to keep the price of labour down. Hansen, Lind and Møller see the workfare strategy as 'a tightening of the work and activity norm' which goes as follows: 'all adults must do paid work or other income-generating work and will hereby contribute to their own and society's reproduction' (ibid: 14).

Jørn Loftager (1998, 1999) also has a critical perspective on Danish workfare policy. He interprets it as a paradigm shift in welfare policy thinking from a universal social-liberal to a new communitarian conception of community. Loftager uses Durkheim's classical distinction between mechanical and organic solidarity and sees the workfare policy as an attempt by the political elite to create an old mechanical solidarity where the essential substance of community is shared norms and values, and performing 'paid work is the invariable top norm par excellence' (Loftager 1998: 11). If you do not have paid work, you are not a real member of the community. Activation creates a new power structure which goes against the principle of the individual's autonomy and integrity, and it creates a new group without normal labour rights and with a special obligation to accept activation.

Where Torfing and Jensen see Danish workfare policy as a success, Hansen, Lind and Møller document 'very poor' results for long-term unemployed in terms of ordinary work or education after activation. Where Torfing – along with the Danish government and OECD – talks about a 'Danish miracle', Hansen, Lind and Møller show that long-term unemployment has only been reduced by approximately 10,000 persons.

Danish analyses of the new workfare strategy lack the long historical perspective in the understanding of the concepts of rights and responsibilities and differ in their understanding of how these concepts were perceived in the former 'Danish' or 'Scandinavian' model.

RIGHTS OF LABOUR: EQUAL POLITICAL RIGHTS AND RESPONSIBILITIES AND PROTECTION OF WAGE WORK

What was the real meaning of the old slogan: 'Do your duty, demand your rights' in the infancy of the labour movement? (Callesen and Lahme, 1978: 100-115, 45-47 and 50-52). The IAA's (the International Association of Labour in Denmark) rules from 1871 state that: 'The Congress considers it a duty to claim civil and human rights, not only for its own party, but for everybody who does his duty. No rights without obligations, no obligations without rights.'

The slogan was turned against the privileges of the upper class, and the goal was 'to abolish all privileges from status and birth'. The upper class had rights without obligations, whereas the growing working class had obligations without rights. Therefore, the labour movement's programme for The Social Democratic Society (1875) and 'Gimleprogrammet'(1876) demanded universal tax liability: 'introduction of direct income tax with increasing progression and higher taxes on land', and conscription: 'establishment of a national army instead of a standing army'. These demands were turned against the upper class. Furthermore, the labour movement demanded certain equal rights, e.g., equal and common suffrage, rights to education, freedom of speech, thought and faith, and freedom of association and assembly. With the demand for rights and obligations, the new labour movements attacked the hegemonic discourse which was a mix of feudal-bourgeois elements.

The labour movement understood the relation between rights and obligations in political-legal terms. To claim a right meant that the state (society) had an obligation to make it possible to use this right. The demand for suffrage did not mean compulsory suffrage, but that the state had an obligation to make suffrage possible.

The new labour movement did not fight for the right to wage work and full employment; these demands came later. Instead, they fought for the right to organise as workers, for state protection of wage work, i.e., a normal work day; for a ban on child labour, on harmful women's work, on Sunday work, and for a 'stop to competition from labour in the workhouses with free wage work'. This was 'workfare' in that period.

RIGHT TO LABOUR

The labour movement first fought for the right to organise as workers and for social control and limitation of wage work. As part of the general democratic movement, the labour movement was successful in its struggle for civil and political rights and therefore became part of a new hegemonic discourse.

Already in 1907, a state-subsidised employment insurance system was established in Denmark. This new institutional structure introduced a new insurance concept of rights and obligations which has been very prominent in the labour movement's discussions. Membership of an unemployment insurance fund meant entitlement to unemployment benefits on certain terms, corresponding to the obligation to be available to the labour market.

From the 1930s, and especially after the Second World War, the social democratic movement fought for the right to work and to full employment as part of a welfare state. A new hegemonic political welfare state discourse was born. The social democratic movement was a major part of the power block behind that discourse, but rather than being purely social democratic, the ideological profile of the discourse was a social-liberal mix.

The concept of the right to work and full employment gained a foothold when the Danish Constitution ('Grundloven') was revised in 1953. §75, article 1 says that: 'In order to advance the public interest, efforts shall be made to guarantee work for every able-bodied citizen on terms that will secure his existence'. But according to constitutional experts, this provision only states a goal and does not give the individual able-bodied citizen a right to a state-guaranteed job.

On the other hand, §75, article 2 underlines the right to public assistance in case no jobs are available or if self-support is otherwise made impossible: 'Any person unable to support himself or his dependants shall, where no other person is responsible for his or their maintenance, be entitled to receive public assistance, provided that he shall comply with the obligations imposed by statute in such respect'. In other words, all citizens have the primary obligation to provide for themselves, and public provision is only a secondary obligation.

In the 1960s and 1970s, the golden age of the welfare state, one element in the understanding of the relation between rights and responsibilities was that every individual has a right to work, and though it was not secured by the Constitution, the state had an obligation to secure full employment. The goal of full employment was, however, linked to the Constitution's self-provision obligation. Another element was the right to universal social transfers provided the existence of universal tax liability.

In contrast to social insurance models like the German 'Bismarck' model and the English 'Beveridge' model, the Danish tax transfer model separated economic rights and responsibilities.

What does that mean? Former economic advisor and secretary of social security, Bent Rold Andersen, points out that one of the most important features of the Danish welfare model was 'that the ties between contributions and rights are almost completely severed. The benefits are financed via taxes and many of them are free. The scheme is based on the broadest possible solidarity: the whole society' (Andersen, 1984: 35). "Earmarked taxes', in which the proceeds from a certain tax are reserved for a specific purpose, are almost never used' (Andersen 1996: 136).

In the social democratic welfare state, individual citizens acquired rights as part of their citizenship, not as contributors to social insurance as in Bismarck's social insurance system. The universal right to social welfare state services builds on the assumption that all citizens have an obligation to pay taxes so that the universal rights can be realised. In that period, the labour movement defined rights as equal rights for all citizens and equal obligations as joint tax liability.

As Rold Andersen notes, the advantage of the Danish model is 'that only the public sector can guarantee that every citizen has access to assistance and services regardless of circumstances. If, instead, the family is the precondition, people with no family cannot get assistance; if insurance is the precondition, only people with insurance can get help; if the local area and voluntary organisations are the preconditions, people who are excluded or who happen to live far away from voluntary aid may fall through the cracks' (Andersen 1996: 136).

DISAGREEMENTS ABOUT THE UNDERSTANDING OF 'THE DANISH MODEL'

Social scientists disagree not only on how to conceptualise the workfare policy, but also about the theoretical and empirical description and assessment of the former social democratic welfare state, labour market and social policy (the 'Danish' model or the 'Scandinavian' model).

Torfing sees the former Danish model as a statist social democratic variant of a Keynesian welfare state (KWS) ideal type, but he does not define the macro welfare-economic conception as a separation of rights and responsibilities.

His interpretation of rights and obligations in that regime is unsatisfactory because he describes it as a system with 'unconditional rights and almost no obligations' in contrast to 'conditional rights linked to obligations' in the new workfare system. Torfing postulates that the former system was 'never really linked to an obligation to take a job or be trained or educated' (Torfing 1999B: 8).

In Torfing's description of the former welfare state, it is almost a citizens' income system with 'unconditional' rights to social benefits. But this has never been the case. The rules in the unemployment insurance system and social assistance system have always required benefit recipients to be available to the labour market and to register as job seekers at the Public Employment Service.

Loftager's description of the former welfare state is both similar and different. He prefers to see the Danish model as social-liberal in contrast to the mainstream tendency to call it a social democratic model because of the decommodifying effects of social benefits. Loftager claims that the Danish decommodification process took place in a more liberal context than in Norway and Sweden due to Denmark's traditionally more liberal labour market regulation and greater respect for freedom and autonomy for its citizens. Loftager finds that British sociologist T.H. Marshall's (1950) concept of universal citizenship corresponds to the Danish tradition of universality in the welfare state.

Loftager emphasises that the unemployment benefit system and the social assistance system 'have always involved such duties', but before the new workfare paradigm, the unemployed only had to be available for jobs under normal conditions. The new workfare reforms have introduced new forms of activation (counselling, job training, education) (Loftager 1998: 14).

Hansen, Lind and Møller's definition of the classical welfare state is influenced by Gösta Esping-Andersen's (1990) concept of a social democratic welfare state. They interpret the Danish unemployment policy during the 1970s and 1980s as a form of 'decommodification' when 'unemployed received benefits for longer periods and activation measures were relatively marginal and mainly aimed at securing access to unemployment benefits instead of the lower level of social benefits' (Hansen, Lind and Møller 2000: 1).

They also mention, without further explanation, what they call 'the classical social democratic principle of disconnection between charge (taxes) and benefit'. They only hint at the important Danish tax transfer system and welfare-economic understanding of rights and responsibilities in which the state is responsible for creating full employment.

The conclusion seems to be that Loftager as well as Hansen, Lind and Møller see 'decommodification' as a positive indicator of the former Danish welfare state, and one that has been reduced with the new workfare reform. Torfing, on the other hand, sees the 'Danish model' almost as a citizen's income model, and to him 'decommodification' is not only a positive indicator or goal, which is why he welcomes the workfare policy.

Mandatory labour or 'Activation'

Today, the Danish Social Democratic Party has abandoned, not only the political-legal understanding of the relation between rights and responsibilities, but apparently also the main welfare economic conception inscribed in 'the Danish model', and the party now only sees rights and obligations from the perspective of the microeconomic exchange and the insurance contract.

The new workfare policy is based on the following principles: 1. reciprocity: you have to work in return for the money you receive from the state; 2. rights are linked to obligations. When you are entitled to income transfer, you have a corresponding obligation to be available to the labour market. On a market, you must give to get, and there is a special link between rights and obligations. But the labour market is not society, something the Social Democratic Party and the labour unions seem to have forgotten.

In the following passage from a programme proposal from 1995, the Social Democratic Party attempts to conceal how the meaning of 'rights and responsibilities' has changed over the past 100 years: 'Since the beginning of the labour movement, obligations and rights were seen as two sides of the same issue. Everybody must contribute if they want to receive', (Socialdemokratiet, 1995: 8).

In the labour movement's infancy, nobody used the principles of 'contributing in return for receiving', 'giving and taking', the way they are currently used in a logic of market economy or insurance.

The fact that social clients of today have acquired both a right and an obligation to 'activation' is an absurd political-legal construction. A right is not normally synonymous with an obligation. Common suffrage is not the same as compulsory suffrage. It is correct that rights and obligations are linked, but as a rule they do not apply to the same subject (individual). If an individual has a right, the other party – the state – has an obligation to ensure that the individual may be able to enjoy this right.

Workers who cannot find a normal job on the market have acquired both a right and an obligation to 'activation'. Where the labour movement originally fought for equal political rights and obligations for all citizens, it is now busy justifying unequal rights and obligations. A political emancipatory slogan has been turned into a disciplinary slogan.

In the new social democratic philosophy, the obligations for the upper class, e.g., 'social responsibilities for corporations', are only moral, not legal obligations. The people who need new legal rights are burdened by legal obligations. Instead, the strong group that should be burdened with new legal obligations acquires new rights (tax reductions and increased mobility); rather than new legal obligations, they are 'burdened' only with moral obligations, which may even improve their public image.

Rights and obligations in various workfare analyses

How does Torfing see the relation between rights and obligations in workfare? He calls it 'conditional rights linked to obligations', and describes the relation as good, fair and empowering.

He can do this because he constructs a picture of a good and a bad form of workfare: a good, Danish, social democratic workfare, and a bad, neoliberal, British and American workfare. The principles of the latter are: 1. 'work for benefits'; 2. 'control and punishment'; 3. 'lower benefits'. The principles of the good, Danish form of workfare are: 1. 'training and education'; 2. 'empowerment'; 3. 'skill enhancement and work experience'.

His conclusion is that Danish workfare, because it is good, restores rather than dissolves the universal Danish welfare. 'The Danish case undermines the myth that workfare is essentially neoliberal, punitive and bad'. Workfare 'disempowers' the client in a neoliberal, residual welfare state, but 'empowers' the client in a social democratic welfare state (Torfing 1999B: 23).

In Jensen's opinion, the relation between rights and obligations has, in some ways, not changed: The obligation to be available to the labour market is the same as before. However, he sees the right to a personal 'action plan' as an improvement and interprets it as a new right. This concept is need-oriented in relation to the clients and gives them a 'positive choice', new possibilities for influence. Jensen uses Giddens' concept of 'life politics' which is 'about new second chances in all aspects of life', and the new labour market policy gives the unemployed and the client an 'action plan', a tool 'that enables individuals to gain control over their lives' (Jensen 1999: 14).

At the micro level, Jensen's analysis sees wage labour as the defining role in relation to self-identity, and at the macro level it sees wage labour as the key cultural value in modern society. Jensen therefore calls the new strategy an 'enabling life policy strategy'.

Where Jensen sees continuity with a new right to an action plan as a room for empowerment, Loftager sees it as disrupting the development of the welfare state because rights are reduced, and a new selective obligation to activation is created. Activated persons have lost their former access to the unemployment insurance system through activation. It creates a new power structure which is against the principle of individual autonomy and integrity, and a new class of people without normal labour rights and with a special duty to activation is created.

Hansen, Lind and Møller agree with Loftager in the description of an asymmetrical relation in the new workfare policy with reduced rights and the dictate of a new obligation to work. They interpret it in a disciplinary perspective and see it as 'a sudden and flagrant break with a century-old right for members of unemployment funds to receive benefits during unemployment. The only condition is to be available to the labour market' (Hansen, Lind and Møller 2000: 14). Their key to understanding compulsory activation is that the workfare policy keeps discipline in the work force, it legitimises a relatively high level of unemployment benefits, and it is a tool for the Social Democratic government to avoid neoliberal solutions to labour market regulation.

How can Torfing and Jensen see improved justice in the new workfare policy? A comparison with the rules and the critical analyses shows that the legitimising approach ignores the reductions in the rights for unemployed and social clients, the structural asymmetrical power relation behind the action plan, and the historical change in the interpretation of the relation between rights and obligations.

Torfing tries to conceal the fact that the Danish workfare also builds on: 1. work in return for benefits; and 2. control and punishment. The Danish and the British workfare systems differ, but the similarities are more pronounced.

When Jensen uses Anthony Giddens' theoretical framework and support of the 'third way' slogan 'no rights without responsibilities', he overlooks Giddens' critical remarks to that slogan. Giddens points out that: 'Government has a whole cluster of responsibilities for its citizens and others, including protection of the vulnerable' (1998: 65-66). Giddens stresses that, 'As an ethical principle, 'no rights without responsibilities' must apply not only to welfare recipients, but to everyone. It is highly important for social democrats to stress this because otherwise the precept can be held to apply only to the poor or to the needy – as tends to be the case with the political right'.

Giddens here describes exactly what has happened with the Danish workfare strategy and the social democratic rhetoric about rights and responsibilities: The new talk of responsibilities is only compulsory 'activation' for the poor.

A difference between the supporters and critics of workfare is that the supporters to a large extent build their evaluation of activation on the intention and goals as expressed in the law and by the political elite who formulated the new policy. Jensen says, for example, that 'in principle, there is no meaningless activation' (Jensen 1999: 14), and Torfing also follows the perspective of the system when he states that 'participation in futile work – for the sake of the work process – is limited' (Torfing 1999B: 18). Jensen's and Torfing's analyses largely legitimise the government's perspective. They lack a critical distance to the goals as they are expressed in the law.

But the difference in their scientific framework also determines the interpretation of the empirical analyses of the activation project. Where the supporters see a relative success, the critics see a relative failure. Both sides admit that the result can be interrelated in different ways. The glasses you wear determine what you see as problematic. Supporters focus especially on the short-term unemployed and satisfied individuals, and critics on long-term unemployment and the dissatisfied.

A NEW UNIVERSAL RIGHT TO A MINIMUM INCOME

The new hegemonic Danish workfare discourse must be seen in relation to an excluded citizen's income discourse in the 1990s, which at the time represented a heretical discourse, and a fulfilment of universal social citizenship in the welfare state (Christensen 2000C). Political discourses can only be understood in relation to other discourses because they must be defined in a mutual struggle in a process of inclusion/exclusion where the hegemonic discourse is developed.

How were rights and responsibilities defined in the heretical citizen's income discourse in the 1990s, and what could a future justification for a citizen's income be? A right to a minimum income could be seen as compensation for all the unpaid, socially necessary work carried out by citizens. And a right to a minimum income should correspond to a joint tax liability.

In modern society, a lot of unpaid, socially necessary work is done in the form of housework, care work, political work and cultural work. This work ensures that the market functions and that the political community is reproduced, and the people who perform this work are not compensated. One can say that these people are 'contributing without receiving'. However, other people profit from this work without contributing to it. They 'receive without contributing'. Or, with a popular social science concept, one may call it widespread 'free riding', some groups are 'free wheeling', profiting without paying.

The structure of society can be described as a situation in which a few persons (who have capital) have freedom from wage work as opposed to compulsory wage work for the majority. Those with capital have a right to an income, which is created by society, but they have no further responsibilities (other than the obligation to pay taxes).

The new citizen's income concept may be seen as a combination of a political-legal definition of rights and obligations, just as in the early labour movement days, and a new formulation of the classical welfare state legitimation with a tax liability.

The Danish social scientists, who discuss and criticise workfare, lack a clear alternative concept of rights and responsibilities in society and on the labour market. Only Loftager directly supports a citizen's income model. He sees citizen's income in the historical perspective introduced by T.H. Marshall (1950) where it is a fulfilment of the development of social rights, but he does not connect the right to a citizen's income with the function of unpaid work. He sees the classical welfare state as characterised by two contradictory norms: a liberal state with equal citizenship aiming at neutrality and universality, treating people as citizens with freedom and responsibility to design their own lives, and a norm of doing paid work as an important part of being a full member of the community.

Conclusion

In this article I have offered the following analysis:

1. The meaning of rights and obligations has changed dramatically in labour movement ideology over the past 100 years. As Guy Standing (1999: 337) points out, the agenda of the labour movement has in this period changed from a strategy for rights of labour to a right to labour and, with the new workfare strategy, to an obligation to labour.

When the Social Democratic Party today interprets rights and obligations within a narrow logic of market and insurance, it not only breaks with the original ideological foundation, but also with the core meaning of the welfare state after the Second World War.

In the infancy of the labour movement, the slogan, 'Do your duty, claim your right' was understood in political-legal terms as a fighting slogan for new rights against the privileges of the upper class (lacking duties). Today, that slogan is used by the Social Democratic Party to justify that the upper class (the permanent full-time workers) can maintain the marginalised (unemployed and social clients) as a second-rate workforce (in workfare) with a special obligation to work for their social transfers.

2. Political discourses are often supported and legitimised by scientific paradigms. In Denmark both the political discourse on workfare and a new political citizen's income discourse are supported by different scientific paradigms. I have shown that the different views on Danish 'activation' in various social science analyses are determined by the different scientific frames.

In frameworks where wage work is seen as the norm and as the foundation of society, the new workfare system can easily be interpreted as an 'empowerment' strategy. On the other hand, in a framework where universal political citizenship is seen as the core of a democratic society, a new citizen's income concept of rights and responsibilities is possible, and here the workfare strategy will be interpreted as a disciplinary power strategy against a new underclass without wage work.

3. All rational political strategies must have a concept of justice to be legitimate, and if it is not possible to go back to classical welfare legitimation, one must develop a new alternative concept. Also, it is only possible to criticise the workfare strategy if one has an alternative understanding of rights and responsibilities, a new concept of justice.

Injustice always exists in the presence of privileges, while justice is characterised by equal rights for all, and former privileges are extended to all. In the contemporary market society, the busiest participants on the market make a good deal of capital on the informal, socially necessary work, which is a precondition for a functioning market, and a small group receives income without wage work. I have argued that if all citizens were guaranteed an existence income without wage work, part of these two injustices would be removed, and a new room for development of the political democracy would be created.

A way to create another ideological and logic order (than workfare) in the social democratic ideology would be to fight for a universal minimum (basic) income (or citizen's income) instead of the hopeless fight for normal full wage work for all citizens.

Feminist Arguments in Favour of Welfare and Basic Income in Denmark

Introduction

The extensive social science research on women and welfare rarely offers feminist political arguments in favour of guaranteed basic income or citizen's income. This is surprising in view of the convincing arguments that large groups of women would benefit from a basic income scheme because it would: (1) lead to equal treatment of the genders on the labour market and in the social sphere; (2) express recognition of unpaid work; (3) guarantee income outside the labour market and thus strengthen family life; (4) give many people more incentive to work; (5) ensure economic independence within the family; and (6) encourage a more equal division of labour in families (McKay & Vanevery 2000, McKay 2001).

Women's research generally agrees that the current Scandinavian welfare states are among the most 'women friendly' societies, but that gender-related injustice still exists. 'There are still fundamental contrasts between work life and family life, and women earn less than men at the same level. In addition, women rank lower than men in the job hierarchy, and they have less power and influence in society than men' (Borchorst 1998: 127). It therefore seems odd that basic income has not attracted more attention in women's research.

Considering that some feminists (Siim 2001) call for new equality and solidarity visions that include women as well as marginalised social groups in the welfare state, it seems obvious to ask why it is so hard for many feminists to see and accept basic income as a long-term, ideal solution to ongoing gender inequality and injustice.

With reference to the debate in Denmark, I will argue that:

1. one reason for the modest feminist interest in basic income is that women's research and the women's movement have been locked into a Wollstonecraft's dilemma, named after Mary Wollstonecraft (1759-1797), the pioneer of the British women's movement (Pateman 1989: 195-204, Christensen & Siim 2001: 19-20). The women's movement has worked, on the one hand, for equality and a gender-neutral society, and, on the other, for recognition of women's difference from men, their special abilities and needs. There seem to be two different paths to gender equity; hence the talk of a dilemma. In modern society, the dilemma is often formulated as follows: Following the path of equality, the women will tend to join the dominant, male wage work norm. Following the path of difference by prioritising women's care work over wage work, women will continue to be marginalised in relation to the men on the labour market.
2. Wollstonecraft's equality/difference dilemma is not a real logical conceptual dilemma, but rather an impossible choice that resembles a 'double bind' defined by the dominant, patriarchal power structure. Like other gender-political dilemmas – commodification/decommodification, dependence/independence and wage work/care – this dilemma can be broken down by a critical, deconstructive analysis.
3. the dilemma can be solved or softened theoretically by adding conceptual nuance to the equality and difference concepts as American philosopher Nancy Fraser has done. She suggests that a universal basic income, or citizen's income,

will fulfil the desire for equality and difference, combine decommodification and commodification, and create a new type of economic independence that could be a basis for new dependence relations.
4. the modest interest in the basic income concept both in Danish and international women's research is a result of a greater focus on increasing women's participation in the labour market (commodification) than on securing economic independence in relation to the labour market (decommodification). In addition, attempts to accommodate care needs have been met with scepticism because they might retain women in the traditional gendered division of labour. Unconditional basic income was either seen as utopian or dangerous in the short term because it might keep some women from entering the labour market.
5. Danish feminists have nevertheless developed theoretical understandings of the relation between wage work and care that open the way for new arguments in favour of basic income.

TOWARDS A NEW BREADWINNER MODEL – BUT WHICH ONE?

The last 30 years has brought about a revolution in the societal, gendered division of labour. All welfare states have abandoned the old 'male breadwinner model' with its clear division of labour between a male wage worker and a female care worker in the family. Many women have entered the labour market, and the family's role and functions in relation to children and the elderly have changed as new public and private care systems have expanded.

However, although the breadwinner model has been abandoned, we can still use it as a benchmark, which is what Ilona Ostner (1996) and Jane Lewis have done (Lewis & Ostner 1994): they created the concept of 'the male breadwinner model' as a reaction to Gösta

Esping-Andersen's (1990) typology of liberal, corporative and social democratic welfare states which has decommodification as the key concept.

They argue that women, and thus the gendered division of labour, disappear in Esping-Andersen's analysis because he focuses on state and market and ignores unpaid work. As a reaction, they constructed what they called a strong male breadwinner model. This aims to define some qualitative and quantitative measures for the degree to which welfare states liberate women from family obligations, i.e., in what sense the welfare state individualises women. They see two dimensions in individualisation: (1) economic independence, i.e., women's opportunities to earn their own money, and (2) independence from family obligations, i.e., society as care giver and women's real choice in terms of care work in the family.

This concept is the basis for Ostner's and Lewis' classification of the European welfare states which distinguishes between strong male breadwinner states (England and Germany), moderate male breadwinner states (France), and weak male breadwinner states (the Scandinavian countries).

The typical male breadwinner model has a clear, gender-dualistic division of labour: the husband has full-time wage work, the wife is full-time homemaker and caregiver for children and the elderly. In the weak male breadwinner model, both husband and wife have wage work which is possible because the state has assumed a significant share of child and elder care, a work that was previously carried out by women.

Danish researchers use different concepts to describe the Danish welfare state from a gender perspective. The Ostner/Lewis model describes it as a 'weak male breadwinner model' because women, according to their indicators, still lag behind men in terms of economic independence measured by participation rate. Likewise, there is a weak dependency in the legislation. The individual principle has been implemented in Danish social legislation to a large extent, but not completely.

Birte Siim (2000) describes the Danish welfare model as a 'dual breadwinner model', or an 'adult worker model', to emphasise that a norm has developed according to which all adults, regardless of gender, are expected to have wage work and be self-supporting. In that sense, the modern Danish welfare state is widely regarded as gender neutral.

Two factors explain the progress in the Danish and the other Nordic welfare states: the rise in the female participation rate, and the expansion of public child and elder care facilities. These two factors are the preconditions for women's liberation from the homemaker role and private care work and their entry into wage work.

Despite the increased equality, Danish society is still far from giving completely equal status and justice in the gendered division of labour. Unpaid house and care work is still not equally divided, and inequality in the labour market is significant, both in terms of wage and jobs. The result is a high level of gender segregation, with a majority of women among the low paid and publicly employed. Moreover, more women than men are unemployed or receiving income transfers.

THE DANISH DEBATE ON LEAVE SCHEMES AND EQUALITY BETWEEN WORK AND CARE

In 1994, Denmark introduced a new labour market policy with three leave schemes: child care leave, educational leave and sabbatical leave. At the time, unemployment was very high in Denmark (12 percent), and the main objective of the schemes was to reduce unemployment through job rotation and job sharing. Another objective was to enhance the qualifications of the work force and improve the balance between family and work life through better possibilities for paid care work (Jensen 2000).

In the Danish gender-political debate on the leave schemes, the arguments concerning the relationship between wage work and care stayed within the boundaries of an equality/difference dilemma similar to Wollstonecraft's classic formulation of women's choices.

The women's movement and the Equal Status Council (Ligestillingsrådet) supported the new leave schemes, although they did express criticism and concern about equality on the labour market. It was also noteworthy that the leading women politicians on this occasion clearly rejected general pay for informal care work.

Two high-ranking women from the Socialist People's Party, Christine Antorini and Margit Kjeldgaard, expressed scepticism about the new parental leave in a newspaper article before the new labour market reform was implemented (Information, December 21, 1993). They were particularly worried that granting a right to parental leave would weaken women's position in the labour market. In their view the prime target should be labour market inequality followed by the division of labour in families.

In that same period, Britta Foged, chairwoman of the Danish Women's Society, rejected pay for work and child care performed in the homes saying: 'I am fundamentally opposed to paying people for staying at home' (Information, October 7, 1993). She was supported by Anne Grete Holmsgård, chairwoman of The Equal Status Council, who said, on the same occasion: 'I don't see the logic in receiving money for staying at home and taking care of one's children.'

These unambiguous statements were made in connection with a rejection of a proposal from the Christian People's Party for a general subsidy to parents who take care of their own children. Interestingly, Foged called the proposal 'of an area the state should not interfere with.' Anne Grethe Holmsgård 'felt bad about turning family work into productive work.' She would like to 'appreciate house work,' which required a 'change in attitude,' but 'I don't see why we have to put money on the table for that reason.'

In 1994, the Equal Status Council published The Equality Dilemma, a discussion anthology (Carlsen & Larsen 1994) focused on dual income families with children in day care institutions.

As already stated, the norm in the labour market often tends to prioritise work life over family life. This goes against the priorities of most women who are thus disadvantaged in the labour market. The objective was to 'introduce new ideas and launch new discussions'.

The anthology's title and preface suggested a dual equality objective: (1) creating balance (equality) between work and family life; (2) creating balance (equality) between men and women in the labour market.

The Equal Status Council's activities mainly focus on the latter form of equality. It remained unclear whether the call for innovative thinking and reassessment of old strategies was aimed at equality on the labour market or equality between family and work life. However, there was a clear sense that gender equality on the labour market was the primary goal.

A specific topic of discussion was whether the old strategies of creating more time for parents with full-time work were adequate: part-time, flexible hours, extended maternity leave. While they may have improved the balance between work and family life in the individual family, they also seem to have led to new labour market inequalities. The old methods could, as the editor of the anthology said, 'threaten the form of equality that preconditions women's self-support through paid work outside the family' (ibid: 10-11). This statement contained a latent criticism of the parental leave scheme that had just been introduced.

Deconstructing some gender political dilemmas

The theoretical debate on the nature of the Danish welfare model and the political debate about the prioritisation of wage work and care demonstrate the need for a theoretical deconstruction and reflection on various conceptual pairs that are used in both discussions.

EQUALITY/DIFFERENCE

Carole Pateman has reformulated Wollstonecraft's dilemma as follows:

'On the one hand, they (women) have demanded that the ideal of citizenship be extended to them, and the liberal-feminist agenda for a 'gender-neutral' social world is the logical conclusion of one form of this demand. On the other hand, women have also insisted, often simultaneously, as did Mary Wollstonecraft, that as women they have specific capacities, talents, needs and concerns, so that the expression of their citizenship will be differentiated from that of men. Their unpaid work providing welfare could be seen, as Wollstonecraft saw women's tasks as mothers, as women's work as citizens, just as their husbands' paid work is central to men's citizenship' (Pateman 1989: 197).

According to Pateman, the patriarchal understanding of citizenship, connecting citizenship with the public sphere (state and market) in contrast to the private sphere (family), makes the two demands incompatible. Either women become like men in order to become full citizens, or they continue their informal care work, which has no value for their citizenship. Escaping this dilemma requires a paradigm shift because the concepts of citizenship, work and welfare must all be redefined.

Ruth Lister (1995) shares this view, but she is more explicit than Pateman in stating that the equality/difference dilemma must be seen as a logical, conceptual and political misconstruction that needs to be deconstructed. She leans on Joan W. Scott (1988) who performed a model deconstruction of this conceptual pair. The problem with the equality/difference pair, as it is presented in the dilemma conception, is that the two elements are often perceived as binary opposites and that there is often a latent ranking in the concepts.

When the relation between wage work and care is discussed from an equality/difference point of view, the equality concept is tied to wage work, and the difference concept to care, which by itself implies a ranking: the fact that wage work is male dominated, and care is dominated by women, gives the concepts a specific, gendered connotation.

In addition, difference is assumed to be an antithesis to equality, and equality is presented as an antithesis to care. However, these are false opposites; the antithesis to equality is inequality and not difference, and the antithesis to difference is uniformity or identity and not equality. Equality does not entail an elimination of difference, the creation of uniformity, and difference does not necessarily threaten equality. So it is possible to join equality and difference, or we can say that equality and difference feed on each other. The demand for equality only applies to certain conditions, and is often based on a desire to protect difference.

Presenting equality/difference as dichotomous choices makes it impossible for feminists to choose. If they accept equality, it looks as if they are forced to accept that difference is its antithesis. Conversely, if they choose difference, they admit that equality is unattainable. Either way, they are punished.

Feminists cannot give up on 'difference' which is a creative analytical tool. Nor can they give up on equality because it represents fundamental principles and values in the political system.

Kathleen Hall Jamieson (Jamieson 1995) has shown that 'double bind' communication and rhetoric remain prevalent in the general ideological suppression of women. She defines it as follows:

'A double bind is a rhetorical construct that posits two and only two alternatives, one or both penalizing the person being offered them' (ibid: 13-14). 'The strategy defines something 'fundamental' to women as incompatible with something the woman seeks – be it education, the ballot, or access to the workplace' (ibid: 14). Jamieson lists the typical ideological double bind arguments, one of which is the equality/difference dilemma (No. 3).

1. Women can exercise their wombs or their brains, but not both.
2. Women who speak out are immodest and will be shamed, while women who are silent will be ignored or dismissed.
3. Women are subordinate whether they claim to be different from men or the same.
4. Women who are considered feminine will be judged incompetent and women who are competent, unfeminine.
5. As men age, they gain wisdom and power, as women age, they wrinkle and become superfluous' (ibid: 16).

A double bind creates disempowerment for those who are forced to choose. They are faced with a quandary, and the only way out is to reject the dominant ideological (discourse) definition of options and identity.

The situation on the modern labour market can, to a large extent, be seen in this light. If women cannot support themselves in the labour market, the only option is 'family support' or 'state support.' However, 'state support' is negatively charged and perceived as a burden, and 'family supported' is old-fashioned and also negatively charged.

How to resolve the double bind? Jamieson has different suggestions, all with the one thing in common that they reject the dualistic dilemma and that they demand a new definition of the choices (in her words 'reframing, recovering, recasting and reclaiming'). In this connection, we could also talk of a paradigm shift which is characterised by a new perspective.

COMMODIFICATION/DECOMMODIFICATION

Another conceptual pair that has given rise to different interpretations and misunderstandings is commodification/decommodification. Claus Offe (Offe 1996: preface, p. x) explains that decommodification, the antithesis of commodification, is a neologism that was created in 1974 in a discussion with Gösta Esping-Andersen. Both have used it since, and it is especially known from Esping-Andersen's welfare regime typology.

As mentioned, Ostner and Lewis reacted to Esping-Andersen's conception of decommodification. Esping-Andersen saw it as defining liberation from the market, and the labour movement's goal in contrast to the employers. It was therefore also seen as an objective for the welfare state and as a special trait of the social democratic welfare state.

He defines it as follows: 'Decommodification occurs when a service is rendered as a matter of right, and when a person can maintain a livelihood without reliance on the market' (1990: 21-22). He later emphasises that the concept implies a choice and consequently that, 'Decommodifying welfare states are, in practice, of very recent date. A minimal definition must entail that citizens can freely, and without potential loss of job, income, or general welfare, opt out of work, when they themselves consider it necessary' (ibid: 23).

In this definition it is synonymous with what we understand by basic income or citizen's income, and he does, in fact, mention a guaranteed citizen's wage as an example of ideal decommodification (ibid: 47).

Opposite decommodification, which is positive, Esping-Andersen places commodification as a negative. He refers to Marx and says it leads to alienation (ibid: 35) and that it weakens the individual worker (ibid: 36). Decommodification is therefore indispensable in collective labour actions (ibid: 37).

Ostner and Lewis point out that 'decommodification' and 'independence from the market' are gendered concepts. Due to the gendered inequality in the division of paid/unpaid work, 'decommodification' and 'independence from the market' are not necessarily positive for women, among other things because de-commodification will increase the burden as far as unpaid work is concerned. Ostner says, 'feminist scholarship insists that commodification is prior to decommodification. In order to be granted exit options from the labour market and respective wage replacement or subsidies, one has first to be fully commodified' (Ostner 1996: 3).

This shows that decommodification can be perceived in different ways. In 1990, Esping-Andersen saw it as an objective of liberation, while Ostner and Lewis saw it as an expression of dependence. Ostner and Lewis talk about individualisation (in terms of economy and norms), understood as freedom from family obligations, with a view to making conditions more favourable to women. Consequently, commodification is seen as liberation.

Whereas Esping-Andersen and Ostner/Lewis are one-sided in their use of the concepts, Claus Offe highlights their dialectic character. He sees decommodification as a fundamental trend in welfare state capitalism that works simultaneously with a contrary commodification process. Capitalism and the welfare state seem to contradict each other, but at the same time one cannot exist without the other (Offe 1984: 153). In Offe's interpretation, the state form implies a structural tendency to create commodification, and at the same time the commodification process also requires non-commodified forms. The labour movement has also been marked by this duality; the movement has strengthened the labour force by working for economic growth and full employment, but it has also supported decommodification by demanding a reduction in working hours. The labour movement has, in other words, attempted to create a dual freedom: both freedom to wage work and freedom from wage work.

This is in contrast to Esping-Andersen who only focuses on the labour movement's decommodification goals, freedom from the market, and Ostner/Lewis who are particularly keen on highlighting freedom from wage work.

Dependence/Independence

The debate about commodification/decommodification as liberation to/liberation from also reflects divergent views on dependence/independence.

Just as Offe uncovers the dialectic and contextual character of the decommodification concept, so Nancy Fraser and Linda Gordon have shown, through a linguistic analysis of the concept dependence, how the words dependence/independence historically have undergone a radical change, and that they have a gender dimension (Fraser & Gordon 1994).

In preindustrial society, dependence was perceived as the norm and independence as deviant. In industrial society, wage work and democracy became the norm. Wage work became increasingly associated with independence, and those who were excluded from wage work were regarded as dependent.

The conceptual pair dependence/independence has been associated with numerous hierarchical dichotomies: 'The opposition between the independent and dependent personalities maps into a whole series of hierarchical oppositions and dichotomies that are central in modern culture: masculine/feminine, public/private, work/care giving, success/love, individual/community, economy/family, and competitive/self-sacrificing' (ibid: 22).

In Esping-Andersen's definition, decommodification creates choice and independence in relation to wage work, whereas Ostner/Lewis see commodification as creating independence. According to Fraser, it is important in the emerging post-industrial society to reshape dependence and create a balance between dependence and independence.

Nancy Fraser's redefinition of and solution to the gender political dilemmas in the welfare state

In addition to her deconstructive analysis, Nancy Fraser has also examined the concepts in the context of other conceptual pairs and applied her critical, deconstructive analysis as a tool in a normative reconstructive project.

Fraser wants to be more than just analytical and deconstructive in relation to the welfare state. While most feminist researchers refuse to be normative or political and prefer to give their research a purely scientific look, her goal is to outline an emancipatory vision for a new social and gender order.

'We should ask: what new, postindustrial order should replace the family wage? And what sort of welfare state can best support a new gender order? What account of gender equity best captures our highest aspiration? And what vision of social welfare comes closest to embodying it?' (ibid: 593).

To answer these questions, she constructs a normative ideal type for gender equity and attempts to measure two political, feminist vision strategies in relation to this ideal.

Two ideal types: 'The Universal Breadwinner Model' and 'The Caregiver Parity Model'

One model is largely based on many European and American feminists' preference, namely the universal breadwinner model, which implies a universalisation of wage work. The goal is to increase women's participation in wage work along with a marketisation and of childcare and care for the elderly.

The other model, the caregiver parity model, is mainly based on the implicit praxis and visions of some European feminists. The dual breadwinner model is more common in Europe than in the USA, and it is therefore a priority to ensure that care giving has the same status as wage work. The caregiver parity model thus attempts to equal care giving with wage work through publicly supported care giving in the form of maternity, parental and other forms of leave schemes and through more flexible wage work conditions for women.

Fraser's definition of gender equity is interesting because it shows how she perceives the dualisms of the industrial society (e.g., commodification/decommodification and dependence/independence) and approaches the two general norms of equality and difference.

She breaks the dualism and double bind situation in the gender political dilemmas through a redefinition process that can be seen as a form of dialectic synthesis or paradigm shift. In practical terms, her method is to dissolve the two mega-norms of equality/difference and replace them with a more complex concept with five value dimensions that contain different forms of equality as well as economic, political and social/cultural dimensions.

1. The anti-poverty principle: the fulfilment of basic needs. 2. The anti-exploitation principle: the prevention of exploitative dependency on family, market and state. 3. The equality principle: the obtainment of a certain equality in terms of: (a) income; (b) leisure time; (c) respect. 4. The anti-marginalisation principle: equal participation in different social spheres. 5. The anti-androcentrism principle: a change in traditional gender norms.

Fraser points out that the five principles may contradict each other and reminds us that there are other important goals in society, for instance 'efficiency, community and individual liberty.' However, she does grade the two political strategic models based on their fulfilment of the ideals (the equality dimension is measured on the three dimensions). She concludes that both models are inadequate, both score high on two dimensions, fair on three dimensions, and poorly on two dimensions.

Fraser's two ideal types for a post-industrial welfare state

	Universal Breadwinner	Caregiver Parity
Antipoverty	Good	Good
Antiexploitation	Good	Good
Income equality	Fair	Poor
Leisure time equality	Poor	Fair
Equality of respect	Fair	Fair
Antimarginalisation	Fair	Poor
Antiandrocentrism	Poor	Fair

Nancy Fraser 1994: 612.

The breadwinner model is considered good in terms of preventing poverty and exploitation, fair when it comes to income equality, equality of respect and equal participation, but poor in terms of leisure time equality and changing traditional gender norms. In comparison, the caregiver model is also considered good in terms of preventing poverty and exploitation, fair in terms of leisure time equality, equality of respect and changing traditional gender norms, but poor in terms of ensuring income equality and equal participation.

The breadwinner model primarily aims at stimulating women to adapt to male norms and specifically emphasises market equality. The caregiver model prioritises care in the family, but has no real goal of changing the gender role pattern.

A UTOPIAN IDEA: 'THE UNIVERSAL CAREGIVER MODEL' WITH 'A UNIVERSAL BASIC INCOME SCHEME'

Fraser suggests that to overcome the contradictions between these two models, we combine the best from the two models and discard the rest. This model is based on extended social citizenship and contains 'a universal basic income scheme' (ibid: 615). It represents a deconstruction of the opposition in the gender roles in both the universal breadwinner model and the caregiver parity model, and thus also deconstructs the opposition between a bureaucratic, public institutional model and a private family model.

In a later version of the 1994 article (Fraser 1997), she names this model the 'universal caregiver model.' The purpose is not only to balance the relation between wage work and care, but also to resolve the opposition between what she calls the 'workerism' of the universal breadwinner model and the 'domestic privatism' of the caregiver parity model. The universal caregiver model puts much more emphasis on civil society and stimulates men to emulate women.

The key is that it is impossible to change a dualism without deliberately changing both elements. Fraser calls her third strategy a deconstructive strategy for many of the dualisms in the industrial society which would include gender.

Fraser does not say much about the specific design of a basic income. She admits that it will probably be expensive 'and hence hard to sustain at a high level of quality and generosity.' Some social scientists worry about free riding which Fraser rejects as a typical male concern: 'The free-rider worry, incidentally, is typically defined androcentrically as a worry about shirking paid employment. Little attention is paid, in contrast, to a far more widespread problem, namely, men's free riding on women's unpaid domestic labour' (Fraser 1994: 615). Basic income would be a good way to stop this widespread free rider problem. It is noteworthy that her reference to basic income in the 1994 article has 'disappeared' in the 1997 version.

Elsewhere, Fraser talks about basic income as 'a fully social wage' (Fraser 1993), and about developing Marshall's idea about social citizenship based on genuine rights so that 'benefits must be granted in forms that maintain people's status as full members of society entitled to 'equal respect'' (ibid: 21). On the other hand, we find the neoconservatives labelling it 'antisocial wage' and the neoliberals 'quasi-social wage', while at the same time advocating an increased obligation to work in return for social benefits ('workfare').

The vision of a universal caregiver model with a basic income is 'highly utopian,' as Fraser says. But when she sees it as 'a thought experiment,' it is because the universal breadwinner and the caregiver parity models are not utopian enough. With reference to André Gorz, Fraser sees the basic income model as implying a radical social change.

OVERTURE TO A FEMINIST BASIC INCOME DEBATE IN DENMARK

From 1992 to 1995 the basic income debate raged in Denmark, but remarkably the idea received no support from either prominent women politicians (as a political discourse) or gender researchers (as a scientific paradigm) (Christensen 1999 and 2000C). This was despite the fact that an opinion poll from that period showed that the idea was widely supported by women and the middle-aged and unskilled workers (Andersen 1995).

In general, it appears that the women's movement is largely locked into a rigid wage work and equality paradigm. On the one hand, the idea that women should be paid for taking care of their own children was clearly rejected. This conforms to the dominant tradition in Danish social law. On the other hand, there was no rejection of the new parental leave scheme that was introduced on January 1, 1994.

There was a clear understanding among feminist scholars that the equality principle on the labour market functioned on men's terms and did not lead to equality between work and care. At the same time, there was a growing concern that the new leave schemes would hurt equality on the labour market.

Many in the women's movement were caught in the classic bind or double bind. As described by Nancy Fraser, they faced a dilemma of a breadwinner model and a care model and were unable to find a new understanding which transcended both models. As a consequence, many prioritised and chose the breadwinner model.

However, some feminist scholars rebelled against the breadwinner paradigm in the Equal Status Council's anthology (Carlsen & Larsen 1994). The basic imbalance between work and family life was discussed in two theoretical articles by cultural sociologist, Lis Højgaard and legal expert, Hanne Petersen, who attempted to determine the nature of this opposition in connection with the issue of gender equality on the labour market.

PRIORITISING AND RECOGNISING REPRODUCTIVE WORK: A CULTURAL REVOLUTION?

Højgaard describes how recent patriarchate theories explain the unequal division of work between the genders; they emphasise the correlation between labour market, family and state and call it a 'patriarchal capitalism' in which men mainly work in production (the economy), while women still mainly work in reproduction (outside the economy). Capitalism is the basic structure and dynamics of society; it is exercised in patriarchal forms, and production is superior to reproduction (Højgaard 1994: 21).

Her perspective is a prioritisation and a recognition of the reproductive work in the family. Based on this view, Højgaard concludes that until reproductive work is ascribed the same social value as productive work, and power and remuneration reflect this, both class inequality and gender inequality will persist.

However, the gendered productive/reproductive division of labour has undergone some changes in modern society, and there is no longer the same unequivocal correlation between women's oppression in the family, on the labour market, and in the state. Inequality in house and care work still exists, but according to Højgaard that alone does not explain inequality in the labour market and inequality in politics. Greater equality on the labour market has thus both strengthened the political roles and put focus on equality issues in care work. Other women theorists find a fundamental explanation of the unequal gendered division of labour in the modern welfare state's mode of functioning which secures patriarchal relations through its family, labour market and welfare policies. Højgaard is here close to American political scientist Carole Pateman's idea that citizenship must be based on wage work as well as the unpaid care work performed by women.

From this perspective, women can only achieve 'full citizenship' if the separation of care work and wage work is abolished and new definitions of independence, work and welfare are constructed. A democratic citizenship must encompass both the content and the value of women's contributions, and it must be defined so that citizens are both autonomous and mutually dependent (ibid: 25). The exact meaning of this statement is not explained.

Højgaard hopes for a 'cultural revolution' to resolve the conflict between work and family life, i.e., that men participate equally in house work and childcare and fight for this right on the labour market. This could be the kick-off for a change in the prioritisation of productive and reproductive work. She describes a push process; the leave schemes give women a position in the family from which they 'can push the men to make a change on the labour market, from where the men – freed from the heavy breadwinner burden – can win rights in the family' (ibid: 28).

BEYOND STATUS WORK AND WAGE WORK?

Hanne Petersen uses different concepts to describe the basic conflict. She applies a historic perspective on the relation between the status-conditioned obligation that regulates care work in the family and the contract law that regulates wage work. 'Status-determined life' (family life) is characterised by inequality and difference and is based on values like care and balance in mutual dependency. This goes against the 'contract-determined' life's (the labour market's) demand for equality, uniformity and standardisation which is based on values like freedom, independence and growth (Petersen 1994: 45). Historically, wage work has always had women's care work (status work in the family) as precondition and companion. Wage work and care work have never been equal or balanced.

Hanne Petersen is more direct and provocative in her analysis of how to proceed with equality. She thinks that, due to the labour market fixation, modern equality policy privileges a few women without really benefiting the majority of women. She therefore asks if we have reached the point where we need – particularly from the women's point of view – to reassess the necessity and the importance of all the work that is being performed in a society, regardless of who does it, or its legal form. In other words, how much care work do we need in a society (and for whom and what), and how much production and other material and immaterial goods do we need? (ibid: 51).

Such a perspective requires going against the idea that wage work is a means of liberation for women (and perhaps also going against the liberation and equality ideals) and against the idea that care work is a private matter which the families – i.e., the women – have to perform in cooperation with a low paid and low esteemed public sector.

She then poses a couple of new questions: 1. Can the contract as a form of regulation, including labour market regulation through bargaining, be subjected to a rationality of care, balance or sustainability? 2. How can the courts reduce the polarisation between family life and wage work life? She does not offer an answer to these questions, and not one word about basic income!

Towards a new understanding of basic income?

Once you have a good and concise problem formulation, you are halfway to having solved your problem in that you already know part of the answer. This is true with respect to Lis Højgaard and Hanne Petersen. They both outline the problem formulation horizon on which basic income emerges as the natural, logical answer.

In Højgaard's case, a new universal right to a basic income will create 'full citizenship.' Reproductive work will become visible and receive the same social value as productive work. Citizenship will have two legs to stand on, and the 'new definitions of independence, work and welfare,' which she calls for, will emerge.

Basic income is also the obvious answer to Hanne Petersen's proposal for a fundamental reassessment of wage work as the (only) means to liberation. It will create the institutional balance between work and family life by redefining the work and breadwinner concept.

Money and care support in the Support Triangle — work duty and care duty

Danish feminist scholars have also developed a broader theoretical conceptual apparatus in which the basic income concept appears as a logical solution, if the goal is equality and justice in the gendered division of labour. Kirsten Ketscher, a Danish legal expert, has constructed a conceptual apparatus to analyse the wage work related provider situation. She describes how rules in the labour market and social system systematically focus on wage work and discriminate care work (Ketscher 1990, 2001). She makes a distinction between money support and care support and connects it with a distinction between the different social spheres (state, market, family), the so-called 'support triangle'. Support is defined as the provision of the means necessary for the individual's survival, and each person needs both care support and money support (Ketscher 1990: 33).

Care support is the work involved in cooking, cleaning, washing, shopping, etc.- in other words, everything we normally think of as housewife duties (ibid: 40). Money support is the activity that aims at providing the necessary funds. Money support has three major sources: wages (from the market), support through marriage (from the family), and social benefits (from the state). Likewise, care support comes from family support, public support and market support. In money support, the labour market is the central source, and in care support, the family is the major source, but public support is gaining ground in both. However, it is important to keep in mind that men and women combine these support systems in different ways.

Earlier, men were in charge of money support via the labour market while women handled care support in the home. In the modern welfare state, money support has become significant for both genders, although many women are supported financially by men for a while. Conversely, many men receive a lot of care support from women.

Money support is connected with a legal availability and work duty in relation to both market and state, whereas care support is connected with a legal care duty in relation to children, and for married couples in relation to each other. But where money support requires personal presence, care support can be handled by a substitute (public child care institutions).

Self-support is the leading principle in § 75 of the Danish Constitution and § 6 of the Social Assistance Act, and when it is not possible, a right to state support comes into effect. For married couples, this self-support duty is supplemented by the mutual obligation to support each other, cf. § 6 of the Social Assistance Act, and for parents, the obligation to provide for children under 18, cf. § 13 of the Child Act and § 6 of the Social Assistance Act.

However, with the increasing participation of women in wage work, the problem of double work has come up: they still have the main responsibility for care support, and they contribute to money support. According to Ketscher, this means that they have been forced to choose between two legal obligations: the obligation in the work contract (work duty) and the obligation to care for their children. The difference between the two obligations is that the work duty, in contrast to the care duty, requires personal presence. Moreover, the obligation to fulfil the wage contract and the obligation to provide for the family are not equal. In numerous cases, the current rules show that 'the work duty' comes before 'the support duty.'

JUSTICE IN THE SUPPORT TRIANGLE: BASIC INCOME AS AN OPTION

So how can the modern welfare state resolve the conflict between the work and the care duty and, based on the support triangle, distribute time, money and care fairly between the genders?

Ketscher does not bring basic income into her analytical model, but Norwegian feminist legal expert, Tove Stang Dahl does. (Dahl 1985 I: 85-93, Dahl 1987). Dahl distinguishes between reciprocal justice and distributive justice. Reciprocal justice has to do with reciprocity and balance between parties, with a reciprocal right and duty as the central element. Distributive justice concerns distribution of values based on an entity, a distributor (e.g., the state) where the recipients are made as equal as possible.

Dahl does not think that reciprocal justice is enough to strengthen women's position in the market. We also have to establish distributive justice. She suggests dissolving the relation between social assistance and wage work to ensure women direct access to money and discusses three paths: 1. Care wage. 2. Abolishing qualification requirements for access to unemployment benefits and social assistance. 3. Guaranteed minimum income for all adult citizens.

She does not see any of these proposals as utopian, but rather as central to the women's movement's active participation in a discussion. Perhaps basic income will turn out to be the unifying idea (Dahl 1985 II: 246).

The basic income perspective thus emerges as a logical possibility of the support triangle paradigm. A basic income would make money support and care support equal and partially remove the opposition between the two. By partially decoupling (as far as basic income is concerned) the work duty from its relation to the labour market, the new element in money support (basic income) would be available to all types of care. Basic income would therefore constitute recognition of care work, which Ketscher is asking for, and ascribe it a value in itself.

Although there are signs that the women's movement and feminist scholars are changing their view on the normative function of wage work, the idea of a basic income has always seemed remote and provocative to many feminists. They prefer to think within the mindset of a labour strategy rather than in an alternative basic income strategy.

Conclusion

My initial claim was that women and gender research as a whole have almost ignored the basic income concept. This is only partially true. Some Danish feminists seem to be breaking with the wage work and labour market fixation in the gender political debate and to acknowledge the systematic discrimination of care work in favour of wage work in the current social and labour market system.

The support triangle paradigm developed by Dahl and Ketscher is advantageous in a basic income perspective because it demonstrates that the only way to justice is to secure women economic independence by giving them a right to money support. Dahl/Ketscher are in line with Ostner/Lewis in their description of how women's work/support has changed from being mainly determined by the marriage contract (the family) to being determined by the work contract (the market). The result is liberation from one type of dependence, but with the creation of a new type of dependence, namely dependence on wage work and the state (transfer income and the inevitable clientisation), a situation they share with men. Women and men now also share the mission of liberating themselves from wage work. The right to independence of family, state and market is not for women only, but for all citizens, and it can be secured through basic income.

The international feminist debate is showing some interest in this perspective. Carole Pateman (1989: 202-203), who has described the modern welfare situation of women as a Wollstonecraft's dilemma, is also one of the few to point out that the way out of this double bind is to redefine the situation, make a paradigm shift with a basic income as a possible element. Recently, Alisa McKay (with Jo Vanevery 2000 and 2001) has argued that a basic income scheme could be an important tool in furthering a gender neutral social citizenship in what is called a 'post-familial' society.

Other prominent feminist scholars are more sceptical: Ruth Lister (1995) briefly mentions basic income as a possible solution to the gender political dilemmas, but expresses concern that it could also strengthen or maintain the traditional gendered division of labour, unless it is combined with other reforms. Jane Lewis (2001) expresses sympathy for the idea. However, she finds that a 'participation income' is more realistic than a pure basic income scheme.

Nancy Fraser's normative deconstruction and reconstruction analysis of various welfare strategies opens the possibility that the basic income concept could ascend to the gender political agenda in the future. She demonstrates how to perform a deconstructive ideology analysis, i.e., historicise and contextualise various concepts (dependence, exploitation, marginalisation, equality and citizenship) by recognising the gendered aspects. Generally, she examines how to cancel and/or unite/balance oppositions and dualisms through a more positive assessment of female roles and concepts and a reassessment of male roles and concepts. She is also interested in finding concepts and strategies for joining the oppositions between the old class interest in a redistribution of resources (creating equality) and the new social movements' demand for recognition of their identities (recognition of difference).

In terms of values, Fraser is contributing to the development of a justice concept that includes the socially gendered division of labour. To Fraser, justice is not only determined by market conditions; it is obviously about creating a certain equality in income and jobs on the labour market, but also about creating autonomy in relation to state, family and civil society.

Fraser's analysis is helpful in developing the political-strategic aspects of the basic income concept. She sees that changes in social institutions take place through a political battle between different political discourses in the public sphere, through debates among social movements, experts and state institutions. She therefore finds it important to influence the women's movement's political discourse on the future of the welfare state.

When Nancy Fraser succeeds in theoretically escaping Wollstonecraft's dilemma, it is because she, unlike many other feminists, is explicitly normative in her theory formation. Whereas Ostner/Lewis' typology of welfare state regimes mainly has a descriptive-analytical objective, but is normatively based on a historic rejection of the male breadwinner model, Fraser looks ahead with a positive normative goal. She is one of the few to offer a new vision for creating the kind of equality and solidarity which also Danish feminists are calling for (Siim 2001).

Welfare Discourses in Denmark from a Basic Income Perspective

Introduction

The paradigm shift in the labour market and in the social policy in Denmark in the 1990s can be found under very different names. Officially it referred to a shift from a 'passive' to an 'active' labour market and social policy. The principles of this new line of policy have been coined in expressions such as 'quid pro quo' ('something for something'), 'work before pleasure' or 'rights and obligations', all of which have been used more or less synonymously.

It is interesting to note how varied the social scientists are in their descriptions of this paradigm shift. Their choice of words, as reflected in their acceptance or criticism of the common sense ideological language, is an indication of which ideological and theoretical perspective they support.

Labour market researchers, who are particularly interested in how the labour market operates, talk about a shift from 'employment protection and support' to 'welfare-to-work and the upgrading of skills' (Jørgensen 2002). In the legal profession where the main focus is the principle of allocation of social benefits, they talk about how 'the self-support principle' and the 'labour market principle' have been developed and strengthened. (Ketscher 2002B). Some political scientists, who are interested in the ideas of the political community, describe the turn as a shift from a liberal notion of citizenship and solidarity to a communitarian (Loftager 2002). Economists, however, who are studying the principles of financing, describe it as a turn from a 'tax-transfer model' to something resembling an 'insurance and market-oriented model' (Jørn Henrik Petersen 1996B).

Nearly all social scientists agree in describing the development as some sort of qualitative shift, a move from certain basic principles to other basic principles. Still they disagree in many respects because they are interested in different areas of social reality and use different concepts. And there is only rarely any interdisciplinary discussion between the various academic disciplines about the welfare state. Economists discuss with other economists and present their diagnosis, the political scientists discuss with other political scientists and make other diagnoses.

Therefore, I would like to compare the indicated change in the Danish welfare state as seen from a legal, economic and political perspective to show that the different disciplines make very different diagnoses of what the problems are, and how they should be solved. The disciplines are influenced by different scientific paradigms and also have an ideological bias. A great deal of social science has played a part in the legitimation of the change from welfare to workfare.

My aims

My paper has three aims:

1. To create a deeper and interdisciplinary understanding of why the various scientific paradigms approach the analysis of the welfare state in different ways? Why do many scientists close their eyes to the gathered knowledge of other paradigms so that an interdisciplinary discussion becomes a rare phenomenon?

2. To discuss the relation between scientific and political discourses on the welfare state. My thesis is that the politicians nearly always base their ideas on economy when they discuss the future of the welfare state. Why is it that there is a hegemony of the economic discourse in the political life? And how is it reflected in the Danish welfare debate?
3. Finally, to look at the different discourses from a basic income perspective.

MY THEORETICAL PERSPECTIVES

In the first part of the paper I will show that through text analysis it is possible to find what the American sociologist Alvin Gouldner has called 'the infrastructure or the background assumptions of a theory' (Gouldner 1970).

Through text analysis of three Danish social scientists I hope to find a meaningful picture of the systems of concepts as used in their theories. Inspired by Kenneth Burke's cluster-agon analysis (Foss 1996) I will try to find the synonymous and antonymous dimensions in the texts, in other words, find the key word and the secondary concepts and see which words are ranked equal, associated, identical or in contradiction to each other.

In general, there is little or no focus on a theory's background assumptions, though they are very important for the use of a theory. These assumptions are conceptions of the basic nature of man and society (the state), the power-relations and views on reciprocity in society. As background assumptions are concerned with some of the fundamental conceptions about man and society, they often 'provide foci for feelings, affective states, and sentiments' (Gouldner 1970: 37).

The implication of this is that scientists – for theoretical reasons – rarely accept background assumptions. Assumptions cannot be chosen deliberately. They are usually internalised, and one can not immediately break away from them. Often they function as relatively conservative stereotypes or prejudices. They don't change in the face of changes in the real world. Rather it is so that any new information is adapted to the already established background assumptions.

Gouldner gives part of the explanation of why there is so little discussion among theorists with different paradigms. He talks about the 'metaphysical pathos of ideas' (1955). It means that a theory or an idea 'reinforces or induces in the adherent a subtle alteration in the structure of sentiments through which he views the world'. Theories and paradigms create groups of researchers who unconsciously form a closed discussion group.

In the second part of the paper, I will discuss the relation between scientific discourses and the hegemonic political discourses in society, and how the hegemonic discourse is maintained and reproduced, particularly in relation to the new Danish Welfare Commission.

The function of scientific paradigms and discourses is, in particular, to create new knowledge and understanding in the scientific society, while the function of political discourses is to create identity, support and coalitions for specific political solutions. Society may be considered a hegemonic community held together by a hegemonic discourse which in its contrasting interaction with other discourses is reproducing and transforming society (Fairclough 1992). On the one hand, a hegemonic discourse is created by excluding alternative discourses, and on the other, by including potential members in an alliance in the public.

State commissions often have the function of maintaining and reproducing the hegemonic discourse. The work of commissions is important for the way a society chooses to categorise its problems. It is through the work of the commissions that many organisations and institutions ensure that the problems are adapted to the problem horizon of those institutions. In this way they can maintain the hegemonic discourse.

It was a characteristic feature of all major Danish commissions in the 1990s that attempts were made at arriving at a consensus between the two dominating discourses: the liberal market discourse and the social democratic discourse. The primary goals of the commissions are to create a sustainable common identity and a political coalition. More specifically this is realised by setting the terms of reference for the commission, by the staffing of the commission and through the professional discourse.

A LEGAL PERSPECTIVE ON THE WELFARE STATE

The Danish professor in law (social legislation) Kirsten Ketscher has provided a legal analysis of the Danish welfare state compared with other types of welfare states and the challenge of EU's social rules (Ketscher 2002B).

Due to the growing significance of human rights in social laws, the normative basis for her analysis is what she calls the citizen-friendly ('borgervenlig') style of interpretation in contrast to the authority-friendly ('myndighedsvenlig') (ibid: 25).

Ketscher's story about the Danish welfare state is that it is changing from a taxpayer concept to a policy-holder concept. This may also be expressed as a movement from a universal to an insurance-based welfare model, or from the Scandinavian model to the continental model.

The Danish welfare system is a tax-financed welfare system (ibid: 46). What this means is that the state functions as a tax collector and that, in principle, all citizens contribute to the rights, upon which the state distributes the rights. This form has the imprint of a mutual insurance. The citizen invests money in the national welfare project and expects that help is at hand when he or she meets sickness and old age.

Ketscher talks about a special type of legal reciprocity ('retslig gensidighed') (ibid: 41). During a certain period of time you contribute to the collective account, and this gives you a right to receive something at another time when you need it, a right to benefit from the transfer payments and social services from the welfare state. The principle of solidarity has a horizontal character (over time), and it is possible to talk about the existence of a contract of generations. Typically you benefit more than you contribute while you are young, while you contribute more than you benefit in the adult life, and finally you benefit more than you contribute in old age.

In this concept, it is assumed that there is a correlation between contributions and benefits in the long term. However, there is no direct connection as in the insurance contract. Everyone is contributing to a common pool in which the compensation payments are not connected to the contributions of the individual, but solely to the needs of the person involved.

In the legal perspective the focus is on the individual citizen's relation to the state. This relation is basically an asymmetric one. The citizen stands as 'a receiver facing a distributor' or as 'a citizen facing an authority'. Therefore Ketscher calls the relation 'unequal' because there is an 'authority full of resources' having 'the power to make very radical decisions' (ibid: 28).

The legal position between the citizen and the authority is determined by the basic structure of the public law, the ruling ('afgørelsen'). It is a one-sided legal relationship in which one party dictates the options for the other party. It is the authority who is in possession of what the citizen wants. And the citizen will be in the power of the administration because of the unequal relation between the parties.

This is in opposition to the basic structure of the private law, the contract ('aftalen') where there exists a reciprocally binding legal relationship between two or more parties, and where the goal is the exchanging of equal benefits. On the market the buyer gets a commodity and the seller an amount of money; each party has something the other side would like to have, in other words, we have reciprocity, exchange and equity.

According to Ketscher, the basic principles of the Danish welfare state are under pressure because they are connected to the national state. There a few preconditions attached to those principles. They are founded on a homogeneous society in which the welfare project has been perceived as a national project. As a result, Denmark is being exclusive, maybe even hostile ('fjendtligt'), to foreigners (ibid: 47). From this perspective, Denmark may be regarded as an 'exclusive club'.

In particular Ketscher observes three threats: EU, the increasing number of refugees and immigrants and problems with a number of young people who do not understand the logic of the Danish tax-payer concept.

EU will be a problem because in EU social rights are obtained, not from being a citizen and a tax-payer, but from being a wage earner. Refugees and immigrants also create problems, because they often cannot contribute to the national economy. The trend is therefore moving towards a system resembling insurance where the labour contract ('arbejdskontrakten') gets a central place in the law of provision. This may result in an increased differentiation of rights and create more inequality (Ketscher 2002A)

In this case, the central relation will not be between the state and the citizen as a holder of rights and as a taxpayer, but between an insurance company and a policy holder. The relation will be more private. It is a relation already known in Denmark in the unemployment insurance fund, the labour market pensions and in the early retirement benefits. It is a change from citizen (taxpayer) to worker (policy holder).

At the same time, the connection with the labour market has received a more central role in the social policy. A workfare principle was introduced with the labour market reform in 1994, resulting in a welfare-to-work programme, in contrast to the previous obligation of only being available for jobs on ordinary conditions.

In Ketscher's story a critical-ironical tone is traceable. One perceives a dissociation from the provincially national when she draws the picture of the Danish welfare state as an 'exclusive club' which acts 'in a hostile way to foreigners'. In this context the insurance-like systems show 'a higher degree of openness to foreigners'. She expects that the rights lean towards more insurance, but there is also a certain concern that this development could result in 'unacceptable social differences'.

Ketscher draws a contrasting picture of Danish workfare policy in the 1990s. On the one hand, she dissociates herself from the very work-oriented turn of the social policy when she describes that clients sometimes suffer from an 'expectation of self-provision', which they can't meet, and that the demand for provision sometimes is grotesque. This demand may clash with another basic legal value, the integrity and dignity of the individual.

On the other hand, she seems to accept the new workfare policy. She says that it builds 'on the idea of an active citizenship, where the individual is obliged to do something for getting help' (ibid: 228). But she does not explain the logic of the welfare-to-work principle.

An economist's perspective on the welfare state

The Danish professor in economy Jørn Henrik Petersen has been a member of several commissions about reforms of the Danish welfare state: The Social Commission (1991-1993) and recently The Welfare Commission (from 2003).

In Jørn Henrik Petersen's view (1996B), the Danish welfare state has a double structure. On the one hand, it is a tax-transfer model which follows the principle 'from all to all' throughout the public sector. It is a picture of the universal welfare state based on citizenship, beginning with the old age pension in 1891. On the other hand, it is also based on an insurance model – in which one is supposed to save before benefits can be distributed – beginning with the voluntary insurance against sickness and unemployment from 1892 and 1907.

This structure has created a tension in the model, and in the 1990s Jørn Henrik Petersen's main concern was that an unfortunate shift had occurred in the balance between the core benefits ('from all to all') and the insurance element ('quid pro quo' – or 'something for something') because the role of the insurance element had been played down.

Two characteristic features of the Danish welfare state have been unfortunate, according to Jørn Henrik Petersen: 1. The universal coverage in the role as citizen has made the human relation anonymous and weakened the individual responsibility. 2. The tax financing ('pay as you go') has hidden the connection between the costs and the financing of the welfare state.

The unfortunate thing about the Danish model occurred, in Jørn Henrik Petersen's view, when the old age pension 1956 ('folkepensionen') and later the full old age pension law in 1964 were introduced, and when the insurance element was reduced in the unemployment insurance in 1972. To Jørn Henrik Petersen, it means that the Danish model has lost its balance and no longer walks on two legs. We had created what he called the 'social security state', some sort of guaranteed minimum income. The welfare state had ended up securing 'something for nothing', and this breaks with the reciprocity which is the basis for social coherence.

This was the situation in the beginning of the '90s. If the universal aspect of the Danish welfare model were to dominate in the future, it could create a possible basic income model, which Jørn Henrik Petersen does not favour. Rather he wants to strengthen the insurance aspect of the model.

To him the tax-transfer model has some disadvantages. It does not build on a clear 'something for something' relation or, as he said, a 'reciprocal relation'. It means that there is no link between one's financing efforts and the benefits received in return. And this fact is a cause for problems of legitimacy of the welfare state.

He also very literally talks about 'an absence of any linkage between the great novel about the project of the welfare state and the many small short stories about the daily life of individuals, which threatens to undermine the welfare state' (ibid: 12).

The strengthening of the insurance part of the Danish welfare model could create greater legitimacy. Contribution to pensions is to Jørn Henrik Petersen a reflection of a more genuine reciprocity compared to taxpaying, and it offers a better protection against political intervention. And, generally, a linkage between welfare services and contribution means increased acceptability and legitimacy.

Therefore the spreading of the new labour market pensions was also welcomed by Jørn Henrik Petersen because it strengthens the insurance principle. In this connection he talks about establishing a 'genuine reciprocity' and 'a real principle of right' (ibid: 26). To him exchange and reciprocity is the same.

A main point for Jørn Henrik Petersen is that social life must remain in force in a reciprocal relation. The mutual interdependence is the basis for the power of social relationship.

However, to Jørn Henrik Petersen, being an economist, our society is predominantly a market society. Man is, above all, an 'economic man', who follows his self-interest. The market is natural, while politics is something artificial, something constructed.

Jørn Henrik Petersen therefore makes a distinction between two forms of rights, an economic and a political: 'A right derived from payment is for many people a right to a greater extent than a right derived from citizenship. A right based on equity, in which obligations and rights amount to the same, is for most people more acceptable than a right which is received.' (ibid: 25). Political rights may be changed anytime by a majority in the parliaments which is why they are regarded as weaker.

With this way of expressing himself Jørn Henrik Petersen says that the economic exchange is more important than sociological and political reciprocity, that the economic rationality is superior to the political and social rationality.

A POLITICAL SCIENCE PERSPECTIVE ON THE WELFARE STATE

The Danish professor in public administration, Jacob Torfing (1999B) has made an analysis of the formation of the Danish workfare-policy. It is inspired by the British Marxist Bob Jessop's (1995) theory about the regime shift from a Keynesian welfare state to a Schumpeterian 'workfare' regime. Torfing uses Jessop's frame to analyse the Danish welfare state in a discourse perspective.

Torfing's analysis takes the form of a story about the Danish job miracle. By the end of the '90s the Danish government – in contrast to a number of other European countries – had success with reducing the unemployment from 12, 7% to 7.9%, while at the same time successfully keeping the inflation at about 2%. Torfing attributes the success to the new welfare-to-work policy, a special Danish version of the British/American workfare policy. According to Torfing, the social democratic government succeeded in developing their own workfare strategy without destroying the Danish universalistic welfare model, but only repairing it.

On the macro-level Torfing explains the development with a regime shift from a Keynesian welfare state to a Schumpeterian 'workfare' regime. The background for this regime shift is the growth of the new technologies and the globalisation, including a paradigm shift from fordism to post-fordism. However, these factors can not explain the changes. They are due to a specific discursive construction of these structural economic factors. Torfing thinks that the new Schumpeterian workfare regime has formed two new discourses, one about structural competitiveness which has replaced a macro-economic steering discourse, and the other about structural unemployment which has replaced a Keynesian full employment paradigm.

Where the macro-economic steering discourse had an aim of correcting aggregate economic imbalances between inflation and employment through fiscal and monetary policies, the aim and focus in the discourse of structural competitiveness are different.

The aim here is to create permanent socio-economic innovation, and focus is on the structural policy on the supply side where the goal is to make the market functional.

There is a similar aim and focus shift in the view on unemployment. In the classical welfare state, effort was made to create a frame of welfare based on redistribution and a safety net in which full employment was aimed at. In the structural unemployment discourse, however, it is considered impossible to eliminate the unemployment due to the structural rigidities on the labour market.

It is the change of those two discourses which is the background for the creation of the new welfare-to-work discourse. However Torfing makes a distinction between different forms of workfare. There is a bad and a good form. The bad is the neoliberal British/American where the principle is: 1. work for benefits; 2. control and punishment; 3. lower benefits. Against this he maintains the good Danish form where the principle is: 1. training and education; 2. empowerment; 3. skill enhancement and work experience.

His conclusion is that the Danish welfare-to-work system rather strengthens than breaks up the universal Danish welfare state. According to Torfing, the Danish case undermines the myth about workfare as being essentially neoliberal, punitive and bad. Workfare makes the clients powerless in a neoliberal residual welfare state but it empowers clients in a social democratic welfare state. Therefore he calls the Danish welfare-to-work policy offensive as against the defensive British/American policy.

In this way his story functions as a clear legitimation of the Danish case, both in relation to the British/American case, but also in relation to Danish critics of the workfare, who, according to Torfing's opinion, overlook the role of empowerment in the welfare-to-work policy.

In a later article, Torfing (2002) looks at the connection between content (from provision to welfare-to-work), form (from hierarchy to network-steering) and regulation form (from rule steering to therapeutic dialogue and social empowerment). The welfare-to-work policy is a form of steering in a new form of state. He says that we have a governmental state whose aim it is to expand and intensify the power for the sake of power, to mobilise wealth, efficiency and order, and to organise the level of freedom for the individuals so that it conforms to the superior strategies of power.

Here we see Torfing as the cynic who has seen through it all, that it is a case about 'a subtle steering thought', without trying to develop a critical position in relation to this. He merely registers that we are now no longer given an identity as 'social citizens' but are seen as 'entrepreneurs in and for our own lives'.

A COMPARISON

Why are these three interpretations of the condition of the Danish welfare state so different?

Above all it depends on their different professional starting point. The legal profession is interested in law in force and in the changes in the rules, in the relation between the state and the individual, the private and public spheres. The interest for the economist lies in the economic efficiency, the relation between contribution and cost including the ability to finance the welfare. Finally the political scientist focuses his attention on how rules are implemented, on who has the power and on what the effects are in the process.

The professional starting point determines the use of specific technical key concepts which are connected with specific dominating theories in the discipline. But all disciplines have different professional paradigms with different opinions on the subject area. For example, a political scientist may support a professional political paradigm (e.g. Marxism or the neoliberal public choice) which means that a political scientist and an economist in the same paradigm are more in agreement than two economists supporting two different paradigms.

Comparison of the various scientific discourses

	Law: Kirsten Ketscher	Economics: Jørn Henrik Petersen	Political Science: Jacob Torfing
Key concept	'Rules', 'values', 'state', 'ruling', 'contract', 'citizenship'	'Market', 'contribution', 'benefits', 'incentives', 'responsibility'	'Network', 'regime', 'discourse', 'steering', rights linked to obligation'
Individual	Citizen, client	Economic Man	Self-reflective entrepreneur
Reciprocity	'Legal reciprocity'	'Market reciprocity' 'exchange'	'Network'
Power relation	State versus individual- unequal	Market relation – Equivalence	Therapeutic relation – self-disciplined
State	State governed by law, responsive state	Liberal – minimal state	Governmental state, enabling state
Types of problem formulations	Descriptive, interpretive	Change-oriented	Explanatory
Problem perspective	Challenge, description of the unresolved problem	Recommendation to solve the problem	Explanation of how the problem has been solved
Normative orientation	Critical-ironic	Political-moral	Cynic-legitimating
Scientific paradigm	Critical normative law	Public Choice	Regime theory, Governance theory, Network theory
The main problems in the Danish welfare state	Discrepancies between rules (in the future especially DK and EU). The individual is under threat.	'Free riding', and 'Moral hazard' 'Legitimacy' 'something for something' is needed	Steering and consensus problems
International dimension	Challenge from EU, no discussion of globalisation	No discussion of EU and globalisation	Challenge from globalisation, no discussion of EU
Paradigm shift	From a 'taxpayer concept' to a 'policy-holder concept'	From a 'tax-transfer model' to an 'insurance model'	From 'welfare' to 'workfare'

THREE STORIES

The main problem for the Danish welfare state looks very different for the three social scientists. All declare their support to the Danish model, but their understanding of and stories (normative orientations) about the model diverge. To KK the Danish model is endangered, but she has no idea of how it should be preserved. To JHP the Danish model is in need of reform, and he has a clear plan. Finally, to JT the Danish model has been successfully renewed, so that his project is to explain and legitimate the actual development.

KK tells a critical-ironical story of how this small homogeneous country is under pressure to modify the welfare model from a 'taxpayer concept' to an 'insurance-like concept' due to our membership of EU. The welfare model has been a national welfare model and must in the future be an international model.

JHP tells a moral-political story about moral decay in the Danish welfare state. Due to the dominating role of the universal characteristic of the Danish welfare state, the responsibility is collectivised by rules of taxation and transfer incomes, and the personal responsibility becomes abstract. He wants to recreate the moral core in the welfare state by creating a clear linkage between contribution and cost for the individual in the welfare state.

Finally JT tells a cynical-legitimating story about how a small reform-oriented country has successfully gone ahead in EU in creating a special labour market and a workfare model. The Danish model has been capable of introducing reforms which have further developed its universal character.

Behind the very different stories, divergent views on the individual, the state and the social relations in society are hidden. The citizen, the market player (The Economic Man) and the self-reflective entrepreneur are driven by very different motivations.

Rights and obligations

This is particularly seen in the various conceptions of the traditional Danish welfare state about the relation between rights and obligations; how the term reciprocity is understood in the three analyses. The concepts of right and obligation are used by several social science disciplines, and for that reason they reveal a number of dimensions. The concepts may be understood in a philosophical-moral, political-economical and purely legal sense, and such distinctions are rarely made in the political debate, nor in the scientific welfare state literature.

The rights of one individual create certain opportunities for action which correspond to another individual's obligation to respect this action which at the same time is limiting his own action. In this way one can say that rights and obligations are two sides of the same coin. When one side is entitled to something, the other side has a duty to respect and allow for it. If the sides are the state and a citizen where the citizen has some rights in relation to the state, e.g. the right to vote or the right to free speech or the right to freedom of association, the relation between right and obligation can be expressed as follows: When the citizens have some rights (given by the state), it means that the state – and other citizens – have an obligation to provide these rights for the citizens and respect these rights (for the other citizens).

A popular political phrase in the public in Denmark (as in many other countries) has been: 'Rights and obligations must be connected – no rights without obligations'. And the new workfare rule has been presented as the first genuine implementation of this phrase. It has been essential in the ideological legitimation of workfare.

But the new concept of both rights and obligations for unemployed to work for welfare – upon the workfare reform in Denmark in the 1990s – is in contradiction to the normal legal language about rights and obligations where the normal situation would be that you don't have an obligation to something that you have a right to.

Some would say that a right is only a right if you have the possibility not to use it. A condition is that you have the freedom to use it.

A clear linkage between rights and obligations existed in the traditional Danish welfare state. Ketscher talks about a legal reciprocity. It must to be understood as a contract of generations in which one contributes through tax payments and benefits when one is in need of it. The rights to welfare benefits correspond to a tax liability.

Jørn Henrik Petersen supports the widespread misuse of the terms rights and obligations in the public opinion which is conjuring up a picture of the traditional Danish welfare state as a place where you can get 'something for nothing', and the new reform is accordingly designed to create a state of affairs where 'something for something' rules.

His concept of reciprocity is totally different from Ketscher's. He makes reciprocity synonymous with the reciprocity of the market which should be conceptualised as exchange (by Karl Polanyi (1957)). By using such language, he subordinates the social and political reciprocity to the law of the market. This is happening when he clearly declares that a political right may be seen as a secondary right as compared to an economic right, and when he says that in a market society 'the virtues of labour and self-support are central', and that they insure that society is conceived as meaningful and acceptable. (Petersen 1996B: 24).

Similarly, Torfing is also supporting the distorted picture of the former Danish welfare state when he talks about an existence of 'unconditional rights and almost no obligations' in contrast to 'conditional rights linked to obligations' in the new workfare system. In doing so, he indicates the existence of a basic income system. But this has never been the case. The rules in the unemployment insurance system and social assistance system have always required benefit recipients to be available to the labour market and to register as job seekers at the public Employment Service. Like Jørn Henrik Petersen, Torfing does not conceive the former Danish welfare model as one with rights and obligations, that is, as a common obligation to being available to the labour market together with tax liability.

Reciprocity

In his application of reciprocity as a key concept for understanding the power of cohesion in a society, Jørn Henrik Petersen refers to the American sociologist Alvin W. Gouldner's analysis of this concept. But it seems he does not understand Gouldner's points. To Gouldner, the norm of reciprocity can not stand alone as the fundamental norm in a society because of the existence of various forms of inequality. The norm of reciprocity has its limits. In another famous article Gouldner talks about: 'The Importance of Something for Nothing' (1973). Besides the norm of reciprocity, there must exist a 'norm of beneficence', a norm of goodness. In this norm there is an obligation to give without any expectation of receiving something in return.

Still, a norm of reciprocity and a norm of beneficence, even put together, can not stand alone as a moral code for a society because 'why should I follow these obligations?'. It is Gouldner's view that there must also be a component which he calls a 'moral Absolute', a fundamental obligation to obey the other two moral norms. To Gouldner, a good society's moral-ideological code always has three dimensions. The norms one by one are insufficient because they will undermine each other. There will always be some tension between them. The discussion about a guaranteed basic income for all is essentially a discussion about priorities among the norms. Most people (like Jørn Henrik Petersen) today see the principle of reciprocity as the fundamental norm of the society, and they see the norms of beneficence as secondary. In a basic income society, a minimal form of beneficence (securing all a basic income) would be of primary importance, and on this foundation a reciprocity norm may dominate.

A BASIC INCOME PERSPECTIVE

How do they all relate to the idea of a basic income? All of them supported the dominating discourse. Ketscher was critical at some stage, while Jørn Henrik Petersen was impatiently pushing the development in the direction of an insurance market model, and Torfing was praising the new workfare model.

Thus all were against a basic income perspective. As mentioned before Jørn Henrik Petersen was a member of The Social Commission (1991-93) which took part in the exclusion of the growing basic income discourse in the beginning of the 1990s in Denmark. The commission explicitly defined its task as one of preventing that the transfer income system would develop into something like a basic income system (Socialkomissionen 1993: 33). Similarly Ketscher and Torfing have explicitly dissociated themselves from the idea of a basic income (Ketscher 1995, Torfing 2000).

All the same, it is interesting that even though both Ketscher and Jørn Henrik Petersen are clearly dissociating themselves from the idea of a basic income, in some respects this idea fits with their scientific frame.

Ketscher is also a critical feminist and has constructed a conceptual apparatus to analyse how rules in the labor market and the social system systematically focus on wage work and discriminate care work (Ketscher 1990, 2001). Ketscher distinguishes between money support and care support when she describes the total support situation for all individuals in a society and connects it with the three different social spheres (state, market, and family – the so-called support triangle).

However, with the increasing participation of women in wage work, the problem of double work has become acute; women still have the main responsibility for care support while also contributing to money support. According to Ketscher, this means that they have been forced to choose between two legal obligations, the obligation in the work contract (work duty) and the obligation to care for their children. The difference between the two obligations is that the work duty, in contrast to the care duty, requires personal presence. And the obligation to fulfil the wage contract and the obligation to provide for the family are not equal. In numerous cases, the current legal rules show that 'the work duty' takes priority over 'the support duty.'

So how can the modern welfare state resolve the conflict between the work and the care duty and – on the basis of the support triangle – distribute time, money and care between the genders in a fair and just way? (Se Chapter 3).

The basic income perspective emerges as a logical possibility for the support triangle paradigm. A basic income would make money support and care support equal and partially remove the opposition between the two. By partially decoupling (as far as basic income is concerned) the work duty from its relation to the labor market, the new element in money support (basic income) would be available to all types of care. Basic income would therefore constitute recognition of care work, which is what Ketscher is asking for, thereby giving that kind of work a value in itself.

According to Jørn Henrik Petersen, the welfare state is placed in a field of tension between a universal element with core services and an insurance element. He also calls it a value layer and an interest layer (Jørn Henrik Petersen 1996A). He knows that the universal element is a century old political and cultural construction supported by what he calls 'the common Danish cosmology'.

The idea of a basic income fits fairly well into this frame because it may be seen as the core service of the welfare state. It builds on the citizenship and the tax transfer model. In Denmark one could imagine bringing back to life 'the contribution to an old age pension' (which was used in Denmark between 1971-82) as a new contribution to basic income so that a clear connection between contribution and performance could be created.

Instead of looking at the universal old age pension as the germ of the decay in the Danish welfare state, it could just be regarded as the germ of a new development, the forerunner of a future basic income. Contrary to what Jørn Henrik Petersen says, the universal tax transfer model must be made stronger than the insurance model, not to destroy the tension between the two elements, but to create clear rules and to give the universal element a higher priority.

THE NEW WELFARE COMMISSION

In the last year, both the scientific and the political debate about the future of the Danish welfare state have been intensified. This took place after the Danish government, in the autumn of 2003, formed a Welfare Commission which was given the task of analysing the expected development and the current possibilities for reforming the welfare system. It is a characteristic feature of the commission that it mainly consisted of economists, while sociologists, political scientists and social workers, who had been engaged in the welfare policy, were not represented in the commission. One of the members was Jørn Henrik Petersen.

The terms of reference which the government gave the Welfare Commission made a frame for the work of the commission. At the same time it defined a particular concept and the solution to the problems.

One of the main problems is the change in the age composition of the population because the future will bring more elderly people and fewer people engaged in active employment. What this means is an increased need for welfare services. At the same time, it is assumed that it is not possible to increase taxes. Thus it is assumed that, to a higher extent, it will be necessary to target the welfare services to those groups who are in most need of them. This is only possible with reforms which increase the supplies of work and employment.

With such a term of reference, the government has already made a diagnosis and indicated in what direction the solutions of the problems should move. They want the universal social democratic model turned into one which is more selective and liberal with an increased implementation of the welfare-to-work policy while, at the same time, giving the whole operation an expert authorisation. What they have in mind are state finances and the strengthening of the market.

This expectation was confirmed when the commission, in spring 2004, presented its first report (Velfærdskommissionen 2004). Here it was established as a fact that, given the expected change in the composition of the population, the costs in the public sector will increase significantly faster than the income in the next 10-20 years, the demand for leisure and better services will increase likewise, while, at the same time, the individualisation and the globalisation will continue to develop. The commission discussed several possible options and concluded that the solutions, which will not increase taxes, point to higher degrees of employment and to the reduction of some of the transfer incomes and the introduction of self-payment for some public services.

One of the problematic preconditions which the Welfare Commission has put into the projections, is that they expect the same type of welfare services in the future (40 years from now) as of today. No rationalisation of benefits (like for instance a basic income structure) or development of new types of benefits (e.g. in the EU) are expected. An important feature in the report is the focus on the negative influence of the high tax on the national economy. Most economists regard high taxes as a negative (problematic) influence because they are supposed to lower incentives. On the other hand most political scientists regard high taxes as a positive influence, a solution, because it tends to create a more equal and just society. Finally, it seems strange that the commission has no trust in the possibility of eliminating the existing unemployment of 6, 5%. According to the commission, it is not possible to reduce the unemployment much more, which is why it is necessary to increase the supply of labor.

The first report from the commission is, in certain important respects, influenced by some of the ideas of Jørn Henrik Petersen. This is for instance the case when it is considered that it is impossible to calculate the price of the several benefits of our tax transfer model. According to the commission, this may result in overconsumption of the benefits. They seem to be free, and this tends to lead to overspending. At the same time it is emphasised that the expression 'rights before responsibility' is a problem in the universal welfare model because it gives the impression that everybody has a right to benefits, and that it is the responsibility of society (the state) to take care of the individual.

SOCIAL SCIENTIFIC CHALLENGES IN THE WELFARE DEBATE

Just before the presentation of the report from the Welfare Commission, a discussion book was published in which 13 dominant social scientists presented their views (Jørn Henrik Petersen & Klaus Petersen 2004). Among the participants were two economists from the Welfare Commission, the chairman Torben M. Andersen and Jørn Henrik Petersen. However, it was a multi-disciplinary book with contributions from sociologists, historians, and political scientists.

Among them there was a notable consensus on the fact that the universal Danish model could come under pressure on several points: 1. the universal benefits could come under pressure, making them more selective, 2. in the future, the taxpayer-funded social system could, to a higher extent, be replaced by insurance market schemes, 3. the high Danish tax burden might be challenged, 4. the high equalisation of incomes might be challenged, and finally, 5. the Danish welfare system as a national system can not be maintained.

However, there is a clear distinction between the economic diagnoses of the welfare state (as represented by Jørn Henrik Petersen) and the diagnoses of the political scientists (as represented by Jørgen Goul Andersen). Where Jørn Henrik Petersen sees several disadvantages of the universal model, Jørgen Goul Andersen is about to abandon the principle of joint and mutual liability in the welfare state by introducing a higher degree of selectivity and by targeting the benefits to the weak and poor. It means that, to a greater extent, the middle class is left to secure itself in the market. Or, with an expression from the British sociologist Richard Titmuss, this could mean 'welfare for the poor is poor welfare'. What this means is that the foundation of the welfare state changes from solidarity to altruism (Jørgen Goul Andersen 2004). However, election studies show that means-tested schemes have the least public support, and universal schemes the highest.

The difference between economists and political scientists in the assessment of the effect of the universal model is clear in a comparison between a group of young political scientists and the commission. (Green-Petersen, Klitgaard and Nørgaard 2004). To the political scientists, the universal model is an advantage because it secures equal rights and prevents stigmatisation. The principle of justice is seen as a basis for fairness and legitimation. In contrast to this view, Jørn Henrik Petersen (2004) and other economists emphasise that the principle of rights at the same time may result in a reduced responsibility. Some economists, who the Welfare Commission makes a reference to (Lindbeck, Nyberg and Weibull (1999)), regard stigmatisation for receiving transfer income as to some extent useful because it may reduce the state costs of transfer incomes. These economists assume that the greater the number of people receiving transfer incomes, the less stigmatisation is expected from receiving them. The principal difference in perspective shows with great precision that it is a mix of professional and political assessments which determines the result. And even in this context most of the governments choose, above all, to listen to what the economists have to say in relation to political scientists. This fits into the hegemonic political discourse.

In spite of the book being interdisciplinary, it is striking that none of the participating social scientists emphasise the existence of permanent unemployment and marginalisation as one of the most challenging problems. In the last few years, the Danish unemployment has been at about 6 %, and to this should be added approximately 3% of individuals engaged in the welfare-to-work programmes. The individuals working for welfare are neither employed nor unemployed which is why they don't count in the official unemployment statistics.

Also, neither the sociologists nor the political scientists, except a few like the political scientist Jørn Loftager, see any problem in the shift of balance between rights and obligations in the citizenship which the new workfare policy has affected. Loftager's opinion is that the welfare-to-work policy violates the fundamental principles of the universal welfare state by imposing on a group, that does not have a normal job, an obligation to move from welfare to work. The group of young political scientists does not see the negative influence of the welfare-to-work policy on the citizenship. In relation to the universal model, they talk about model-conform and model-destructive reforms. And the welfare-to-work policy reform is not mentioned as a model-destructive reform; while a potential means-testing of the child benefit is regarded as a model-destructive reform.

Furthermore, they draw attention to the fact that the universal characteristic of the Danish welfare state of today is the universal service (e.g. education and health) while the Danish transfer system in recent years has moved away from the Scandinavian model and in the direction of what the Swedish sociologists Walter Korpi and Joachim Palme (1998) have called a basic security model which is different from the universal model in that the compensation level for people with an average income is relatively low.

Conclusion

What has this comparative analysis of the different scientific discourses demonstrated?

Every perspective has its strengths and weaknesses, because they, one by one, focus on only one part of reality and are blind to other areas. What is not treated in a work is as theoretically significant as its explicit assumptions and hypotheses. Every perspective has its home domain. Every theory is influenced explicitly or implicitly by the particular picture of society (deep metaphors) which the theory contains. Is society perceived as a kind of market or is it foremost seen as a democratic community? Herein are also embedded different roles for the individuals.

These more or less hidden background assumptions have great influence on the diagnoses of the problems of the actual welfare state.

To have a real dialogue between different types of social sciences, a critical self-reflective orientation is needed, both in the academic discussion and when scientists come up with political recommendations on the basis of their research.

The trend is going towards a hegemonic discourse increasingly influenced by a neoliberal economic discourse. And in the hegemonic discourse there is a tendency to adapt the problems to the institutions, instead of developing the institutions upon a new conception of the problems involved. A basic income perspective would be able to reflect this.

The dominance of the economic perspective has, as one of its consequences, that the perspectives of the legal, sociological and political sciences are suppressed in the political-administrative debate. The citizenship perspective, in particular, suffers from this suppression. In Denmark it is reflected in the staffing of the central commissions on welfare policy in which the economists have dominated. At the same time it is worth noticing that many economists don't perceive their participation in commissions as political. (Kærgård 1997). They consider their work objective and neutral, a work directed at helping the politicians in improving the basis for making decisions.

They don't perceive their work as a part of the production of a hegemonic political discourse which is excluding other professional and political discourses.

If a basic income perspective shall gain more support in the future, both in the academic world and in the public opinion, a change in the general political neoliberal climate must take place. A significant step would be if the economists' expert monopoly could be broken in relation to the work in public commissions. It would require that politicians, to a much higher extent, would start using other social scientists for advice, and that they would stimulate a much more pluralistic democratic debate between scientists, the common public opinion, and the politicians.

This, however, would also presume that both sociologists and political scientists were much more offensive and visionary. Today, many political scientists adapt to the economists' supremacy, and they have no visions for the development of the citizenship. Like the economists, they function as tools for the political rulers, just in their own manner. Technically, they provide the politicians with models and arguments for making 'reforms' (e.g. cuts in the existing universal model). Instead, it is desirable that they focus on how it may be possible to develop the universal elements in the Danish welfare model.

A Global Ecological
Argument for a Basic Income

Introduction

Why is an Unconditional Basic Income (UBI) desirable? Basic Income can be argued from very different normative perspectives. One type of normative argument, which comes in various forms, is that basic income may be regarded as a factor in creating real freedom in society. It is a freedom which may, at the same time, be conceived positively (a freedom to) and negatively (a freedom from) because it means that every citizen is guaranteed a certain amount of economic resources. Another type of normative argument is that basic income may be regarded as a further development or consolidation of democracy. Basic income may be viewed both as the fulfilment of the social citizenship and as the beginning of an economic citizenship, and it is not just any right, but a basic right which is a precondition for the exercise of other rights. Finally, there is a third type of normative argument for basic income making it an element in a fair redistribution of resources. This view may be interpreted as an extension of a Rawlsian perspective in which the goal is to secure the possibility for equal freedom for all citizens in a national state, but it may also be seen in the global perspective of sustainable development.

It is this last perspective which I will argue for. This perspective includes a concept of justice which, by adding the three factors of nature, generation and global equality, points to ecology and sustainability as normative arguments for basic income.

What then are the ecological arguments for a basic income? In what way could the right to an unconditional basic income be considered a particular ecological measure and ecologically beneficial in relation to the current social and labour market system?

It may at first appear unlikely with a direct connection between a situation in which a system of transfer payments is changed to one of basic income, and a situation where people would opt for a more ecological lifestyle. Why would people change behaviour in relation to consumption and work just because they are guaranteed a basic income, compared to a situation in which they are guaranteed a support when they are unemployed, provided they are looking for work? If one wants to argue for such a connection, a more detailed explanation is needed where the close connection between particular types of income is put in a larger economic and ecological macro perspective.

The American economist Herman E. Daly has created a paradigm for a *steady state economy* which I will analyse to understand his concept of basic income as an element of sustainable development.

My conclusion is that Daly's arguments for a basic income must be developed by adding a better defined generational and global dimension. My general thesis about the relation between the different arguments for a basic income is that the global ecological justice perspective must have the highest rank as a superior normative horizon forming the scope for the other arguments for a basic income.

An ecological-economic pioneer

The American economist Herman E. Daly is one of the key inventors of the new growing paradigm of ecological economy. The basic feature of the new paradigm is found in Daly's first scientific article in 1968 ('On Economics as a Life Science') and in his first book about steady state economy from 1973 (*Toward a Steady-State Economy*). The paradigm was further developed in books and articles in the following years. In a book authored together with theologian John B. Cobb Jr. in 1990 (*For the Common Good*) and in his most recent book from 1996 (*Beyond Growth*), he has given his paradigm a more theoretical dimension through a comprehensive critique of the dominant neoclassical growth paradigm and developed a theory about a sustainable economy for development.

THE DEVELOPMENT OF THE ECONOMY FROM A MEANS TO AN END IN ITSELF

In what follows, I will demonstrate that Daly's argument for proposing an unconditional basic income as a new mechanism for distribution in a steady state economy is that it opposes the logic of growth which is built into the whole economic system and accordingly into the labour market and transfer system of the traditional welfare state. The thesis is that in the ideology about full employment, and in the mechanism and instruments which support it, a forceful growth imperative is incorporated which a mechanism of basic income would weaken.

The background for Daly's presentation of an alternative to the existing growth economy is a result of his concept of economy and science in general. The world is confronted with a number of fundamental problems that need political and scientific solutions. He observes four positive feed-back loops that need to be broken: economic growth, population growth, technological change and a pattern of income inequality which seems to be self-sustaining and polarising. There is a need for an ecological humanism to create an economy in which economic and population growth are halted, technology is controlled and gross inequalities of income are done away with.

The steady state economy is an answer to this challenge. According to Daly, the economic science must be understood as an instrument, a tool for solving the most urgent social problems. Science should never be an end in itself, but must always be a means, conscious or unconscious, to attaining higher social ends. In line with this argument, Daly looks upon his forming of a new ecological understanding of economy as a continuation of the Aristotelian concept of economy. Economics has its origin in the Greek word for household, *oikos*, implying that one should put one's house in order with regard to resources. It was seen as part of social life and woven together with ethics and politics with the view of creating a good society. To Aristotle, man becomes a being in relation to a community; he is only able to realise himself in a society. The highest end is the manifestation of virtue in the good society. Furthermore, society can only exist if it is materially self-sufficient and built on some form of justice, thereby giving everyone the opportunity to succeed in commonality. I leave out of consideration Aristotle's view on women and slaves.

Aristotle distinguished between two forms of economics: A good, natural form, *oikonomia* "which is the management of the household so as to increase its use value to all members of the household over the long run." (Daly 190: 138). However, economics may also assume another, unnatural form, chrematistics, in which economics is an end in itself. It is the part of the political economy which is concerned with the manipulation of property and capital with the view of maximising the short-term profit for the owner. This dual concept of economics has been lost in the last 100 years. Economics has more and more been considered an end in itself. Along with the development of the capitalistic society and the specialisation of science, economy, in the sense of 'material production by human beings', was separated from its origin in society and nature. Nature and society were established as constants, 'other things being equal', and the work in the economic science was concentrated on the development of models to understand and explain the economic allocation and growth in society. This could only take place because man as well as nature were in practice increasingly commodified, which in turn led to a loss of sense of the unique qualities of man as a being of a vulnerable nature. With the division of labour in science, the field of vision was reduced, while the sense of limitation was lost.

Subsequent to the breakthrough of the natural sciences in conjunction with the industrial revolution, physics stood as the prototype of science. Physics also served as the model for the economic science. Mathematics was not merely regarded as the basis for physics, but for the other sciences as well. This was the background for the American economist Walter A. Weisskopf's (1979) apposite metaphor when he referred to the classical and neoclassical economy as the 'Newtonian' paradigm. It was the same model as the one known from classical physics for the solar system or for the movements of a clock. The economy was construed to be a closed system, the dynamics of which were independent factors coming from without, while the system itself was self-regulated, moving in the direction of equilibrium.

In retrospect, the independence of economics, both in reality and theory, may be regarded as a necessary liberation from restrictive and religious norms and as necessary for economic growth and for the legitimacy of a new capitalist form of production. The new mechanical root metaphor for the economy had both advantages and disadvantages. Daly does not one-sidedly dwell on the negative aspects but also considers the liberating effect of the new model in the social context of his own time: 'Economics contributed to freeing individuals from hierarchical authority, as well as to providing more abundant goods and services' (Daly 1990: 6). Daly also has an eye for the liberating effect of the market society in a specific historical context.

In modern society, plagued with great environmental problems as it is, the machine metaphor is inexpedient if the economic science is to be used for analysing and solving the basic social problems.

As opposed to the machine metaphor, Daly uses an 'organism metaphor or a life metaphor' (Daly 1968) and maintains that the similarity between biology and economics is of crucial importance. It is, for example, useful to compare the economic process with the regeneration and decomposition of matter in the metabolic process as well as the steady state and evolutionary aspects of both biology and economics. An increase in throughput of matter and energy can never be a goal in itself, as the finite physical output of the economic process is waste, something which it is not rational to maximise.

According to Daly, it is fundamental to distinguish between a money economy (consisting of exchange value) and a real economy (consisting of use value), thereby eliminating the narrow 'machine metaphor' which, ignoring the real economy, only looked at the money economy. The economic process is dual. It consists of a circular stream of exchange values coupled together with a linear psychical stream of matter-energy which is not circular. Both of these processes are connected to one another, but can not be reduced to each other. The two concepts for economics (use and exchange value) are both abstractions from the same reality and explain different things. If economics is regarded as a matter of circulation of money without the physical-ecological aspect, something is left out of the equation. If the physical-ecological aspects are included, other questions arise.

The economic process as a physical-economic process may be described as a process in which matter/energy changes state from one of low entropy to one of higher entropy. What happens in the economic process is that free energy is transformed into less free, bound energy, so that the total amount of entropy is increased. The introduction of entropy into economics implies that scarcity must be conceived in a new way. Established economics only knows a relative concept of scarcity, but entropy introduces an absolute concept of scarcity. If the physical side is prioritised, there is an awareness of the physical limits of the economy. On the other hand, if the physical side is not emphasised, there is no awareness of the limits to the scale of the economy, and the GNP is regarded as a measure of wealth. Additionally, if there is an understanding of the physical limits for growth, there is also an awareness of the distribution problems in connection with the economic process, whereas the distribution problem is less important in the event that there is a belief in limitless growth.

Daly uses two basic models (metaphors) for understanding economy. First, 'an empty world economy': economy is thought like a box suspended in boundless space and with unlimited input and output between the two environments, and second, 'a full world economy': a box within a bigger box, meaning limited input and output because of gradually increasing pollution and wear in a more confined environment. This is a model where the economy is seen as part of a system limited by a finite eco-system.

SUSTAINABLE DEVELOPMENT AS A NEW SUPERIOR END FOR ECONOMICS

What is new in Daly's paradigm is the fact that he argues that the idea of economic growth must be replaced by the idea of sustainable development. Sustainable development consists of three different political goals: ecological sustainability, social justice and economic efficiency, all of which are answers to basic problems in an economy.

Ecological sustainability raises the question about scope and is concerned with the limits of an economic system in relation to a surrounding ecological system. This is not accepted in mainstream economics as a problem of economics, as there is no notion of a 'full world', i.e. an ecological system as a closed system. The problem of sustainability can't be solved by the market alone. It is a political problem.

The problem of social justice is how to implement a just distribution between various receivers of income and across generations.

This too is not a problem for the market to solve, but must be dealt with politically from ideas about justice and sufficiency.

Finally, the problem of economic efficiency is one of allocation, in other words how an efficient allocation between the various factors of production may take place. This problem may be solved by the market because of its efficiency in providing the necessary information and initiative.

In the economic theory, it has been recognised that there is, at the same time, a problem of efficiency and a problem of justice, but the problem of sustainability has so far not been recognised. Daly's innovation is his claim that these three goals require three independent political institutions and that the problems of sustainability and justice must be solved politically, while the problem of efficiency may be solved by the market.

In the growth economy all three problems are thought to be encompassed by market thinking. There are no distinct political limits for scope or any norms for distribution. The market evolves anarchistically with only occasional compensations for the negative effects of the market on the environment and the distribution. It is a picture of a reactive political system which only reacts after the market has played its role. Against this, Daly presents an active preventive political system, establishing limits for both scope and distribution with a view to improving the market.

The definition of a Steady State Economy

Daly's concept of steady state economics is a physical concept. It is an economy with constant stocks of people and products created by people (physical wealth) kept at the desired level with the least possible flow of matter and energy for maintaining the chosen stock of people and products.

What usually happens with an ordinary economic growth process is that one attempts to increase utility, both by increasing the flow and the stock. However, any attempt to maximise utility in a steady state economy must take place at the chosen stock level, so the efficiency of maintaining this level must be secured by technological advancements in minimising the flow. Steady state economics requires other institutional structures than is the case with growth economics for fulfilling the goals of sustainability, satisfaction of basic human needs and social justice. There must be established: 1. an institution for stabilisation of the stocks of capital, 2. an institution for stabilisation of the population, 3. an institution for distribution leading to a reduction of inequality.

Sustainability can only be achieved if political limits for the flow of matter and energy from nature into the economic system are fixed, allowing the capital stock to be stabilised. It is a political decision on what level the capital stocks in society should be established. Quotas for the use of various natural resources must be set by political decisions, and subsequently it will be left to the market to allocate these quotas of matter and energy.

Additionally, Daly proposes an institution that may secure stabilisation of the population by introducing transferable birth licences. Justice can not be created by the market; instead, it must be created through the establishment of political norms for minimum incomes together with limits for maximum capital.

Connections between sustainability and social justice

According to Daly, the three mentioned institutions are linked together. The institution for resource quotas cannot be conceived without a complementary institution for distribution. It will in itself sharpen the conflict between labour and capital. Furthermore, an institution for distribution requires limitations on the population.

In general, one might say that the increasing importance of the distribution problem is closely and logically connected with the attempts at finding a solution to the growth problem: 'And we will not be able to shift from growth to steady state without instituting limits to inequality.' (Daly 1996: 215). Considerations on a basic income must necessarily be connected with parallel notions about a maximum income: 'In a steady state, if the rich get richer the poor must get poorer, not only relatively, but also absolutely' (ibid: 214).

Growth may be regarded as an attempt at concealing the distribution problem and failing to take it seriously. Or, it may be put like this: growth is the easy way of out of the distribution problem and the struggle about distribution. As long as everyone gets a little more, it is considered acceptable that inequality continues to exist.

Daly's conception of basic income is closely related to his view on justice as a higher goal than equality. Unlimited inequality is unacceptable. As such, society will loose its power of coherence. However, complete equality is not desirable either; it would be tyrannical, failing to allow for the differences between people. Limited inequality is necessary and fair, and it is guaranteed by a basic income.

'The goal for an economics of the community is not equality, but limited inequality. Complete equality is the collectivist's denial of true differences in community. Unlimited inequality is the individualist's denial of interdependence and true solidarity in community' (Daly 1990: 331).

How should we understand Daly's three institutions? Daly says that they are conservative: 'these institutions build on the existing bases of price system and private property and are thus fundamentally conservative' (Daly 1977: 51). On the other hand it may also be argued that with his politically fixed limits for scale and income he is imposing new limitations on the market, and this has met with the objection that the stationary state is a plan-ecological system. Daly himself asserts that it is neither capitalistic nor socialistic, regarding it instead as a third model. Both capitalism and socialism have agreed about the importance of growth.

The institutions, as conceived by Daly, will allow for stability on the macro-level while securing variability on the micro-level.

By setting limits and controls on the macro-level, room is created for indefiniteness, innovation and freedom for individuals on the micro-level. In this sense it might be said that steady state economics represents a dynamic economy as there is in fact more room for variation and innovation than in a growth economy. With growth, part of the change is purely quantitative, while the change in steady state economics must, to a higher extent, be qualitative.

DALY'S SPECIFIC IDEAS ABOUT A GUARANTEED MINIMUM INCOME: A POSITIVE INCOME TAX

In his book, *For the Common Good* (1990), Daly puts forward a number of ideas about the role of labour in future society and of how a minimum income system should be designed. As the Marxists before him, he is critical of a total commodification of labour. 'An economics for community supports this resistance to the commodification of labour.' (ibid: 299). But he also sees a common interest between Capital and Labour in a well-functioning business community. Thus he proposes a change in the structure of property and an extensive democratisation of the economy so that this common interest might be further developed (ibid: 303). Everyone should be guaranteed a minimum income. In Daly's view no one should be forced to take a job he finds inappropriate, but everyone should have the opportunity to get a job (ibid: 313). Daly makes a specific proposal as to how the tax and subsidy system could be formed. He supports the idea of a negative income tax which has previously been proposed in USA by George Stiegler (1946) and Milton Friedman (1962) with some modifications among which are the taxing of capital gains. For this reason he calls his tax proposal 'The Positive Income Tax'. His general claims to a tax system are:

> A preferred system should: 1. require that the truly basic needs of all be met. 2. be simple and inexpensive to implement. 3. require a minimum of

information from recipients and impose a minimum of special conditions upon them, and 4. provide a strong incentive to work. (ibid: 316).

He examines all specific technical and political objections to the proposal and admits that some of them have substance. It is not possible to change a tax system overnight (Daly 1990: 323). Still, he believes that it is important to design a more logical and consistent system guided by a few transparent and overall political goals.

Discussion of Daly's normative foundation

The normative structure of a theory is determined by the theorist's conception of man and nature. What are Daly's ideas? Daly's arguments for a basic income are based on a holistic human-ecological conception of man and his most basic needs: a human being is a social creature, and nature has a value in itself and has absolute limits. This is contrasted with the mainstream utilitarian concept of man and nature in the growth society featuring unlimited needs and unlimited nature. Daly's conception of man and nature contains a number of values on which the steady state economy is founded:

> In sum, the moral first principles are: some concept of enoughness, stewardship, humility, and holism. (Daly 1977: 47).

The concept of a steady state has been developed by simple deduction from these moral basic principles. Now, what are the implications of those principles for the setting of biophysical, ethical and social limits to growth, as proposed by Daly? What normative arguments does he use when he defends those ecological and distributive limits to economic growth?

First, Daly's premise is that the problem of scale in economics in relation to nature and the problem of distribution are to be solved politically, collectively and not at the level of the individual because those problems involve social collective considerations and operate within another time horizon. While in the mainstream economy the question of scale and distribution is part of the allocation problem, these three problems are, in Daly's view, independent and require three different political instruments. There is a principal difference between an individual, utilitarian valuation and a collective, political valuation. But what sort of ethics is behind Daly's political arguments? As to the question of the optimum scale where both anthropocentric and biocentric positions are possible options, Daly supports the latter (Daly 1996: 51-52). The anthropocentric optimum is fixed according to a cost-benefit analysis in such a way that man's marginal value of using nature corresponds to the marginal cost of this use. In contrast, a biocentric optimum goes beyond the instrumental view and is based on the idea that other creatures have an intrinsic value independent of the use value for man. To this Daly adds a political evaluation of the limits, entropy and interdependence of the ecosystems. Daly's biocentric vision also supports the principles of deep ecology (Daly1990: 203-206), though he dissociates himself from the idea of biocentric equality and argues that a man has greater intrinsic value than a mosquito or a bacteria.

When the scale of the economy is fixed (within the ecological limits), room has been made for distribution. What are Daly's normative arguments for distribution? In his first book on the steady state economy, he referred to John Stuart Mill's view on private property as a protection against exploitation and to John Locke's liberal view on property rights.

> Thus such a distributist policy is based on impeccably respectable premises: private property, free market, opposition to welfare bureaucracies and centralised control. It also heeds the radicals' call of 'power to the people' since it puts the source of power, namely property, in the hands of many people, rather than in the hands of the few capitalist plutocrats and socialist bureaucrats. The concept of private property here adopted is the classical view of John Locke. (Daly 1977: 54–55).

Here Daly is in support of classical liberal arguments for a basic income by granting everyone property rights. But he also points out that property rights, rather than being a guarantee against exploitation, may be an instrument for it, if some own much and others very little. Property rights can only be made legitimate if inequality is limited.

Daly also evaluates the utility of growth in his reasoning for setting ethical-social limits to it when he weighs the benefits of growth against the cost. It is the situation with the accelerating use of the geological capital where the current benefits must be weighed against the cost for future generations. He criticises the general use of a discount rate where the value of the future is ascribed little or no value. In his view the current basic needs of man must be prioritised over future basic needs, while future basic needs must be prioritised over current luxury needs.

To summarise, Daly's argument for a basic income is only indirectly ecological in that he argues for it by introducing the idea of limiting the economy's physical scale and by setting limits to both a maximum income for wealth and a minimum income (basic income). From Daly's point of view, there are different normative arguments for a basic income. It may be viewed from the point of view of basic needs where the basic income meets the basic needs. But Daly also argues from a property point of view where basic income is a way of distributing property to all citizens as a protection against coercion and exploitation from the state and the market.

An additional ecological argumentation for basic income

Does the steady state economy as presented by Daly constitute a satisfactory set of ecological arguments for a basic income, or, if not, what are its deficiencies? First, the steady state economy is an analysis of the economy made from within the framework of the nation state, even though Daly's perspective on such issues as resource quotas is global. In addition to this, Daly seems to lack a more direct connection between basic income and the ecological limits. The ecological limits are secured by a physical system of quotas which is fixed politically and managed by companies. The citizens receive an income in funds, and no connection is drawn to the physical limits. Finally, the steady state approach has been made exclusively from an economic point of view. The political dimension is left out.

If limits to economic growth are accepted as a premise, as Daly suggests, how then should democracy be formed? What new jobs will be made? And what will the ecological citizenship look like?

In order to make up for the deficiencies in the theory, inspiration may be brought in from other ecological theorists. The English political scientist Andrew Dobson (2003) has analysed the impact of the ecological problems on the citizenship and the democracy. Citizenship is concerned with citizens' rights and obligations in a political community. Dobson thinks that an ecological citizenship is different from both the classical liberal and the republican citizenship. Due to the global nature of the ecological problems, the ecological citizenship must be cosmopolitan, that is, with no territorial limits. The ecological citizenship is similar to the republican in focusing on the common good which is sustainable development on a global level. In addition to this, it must hold other rights and obligations than the normal national citizenship which include obligations such as taxes and conscription. As opposed to both the traditional liberal and republican citizenship where the citizenship is understood as a contract between the individual and the nation state and where there is a clear distinction between a private and a public sphere, the ecological citizenship is also related to the private sphere and contains an obligation, not only to the nation state, but also between the citizens. The ecological citizenship contains the same virtues as the liberal (e.g. an open and free debate) and the republican (the common good (sustainability)). But the central virtue is, to Dobson, a new global justice (an equal distribution of the ecological footprint). Dobson's position is that the ecological challenge requires both a right and an obligation to an ecological footprint within the global sustainable limits. The expression 'the ecological footprint' was formed by Mathias Wackernagel and William E. Rees (1996) in order to make the concept 'sustainable development' more instrumental. It is based on an estimate of the amount of biologically productive land and sea area needed to regenerate (if possible) the resources which a human population consumes and to absorb and render harmless the corresponding waste, given prevailing technology and current understanding. In 2003, the average biologically productive area per person worldwide was approximately 1.8 global hectares (gha) per capita. The U.S. footprint per capita was 9.6 gha, and that of Denmark 5.8 gha per person, whilst in China it was 1.6 gha per person. In 2003 the capacity of the biosphere was exceeded with about 25% (WWF 2006). The rich countries use and seize a much bigger part of nature to maintain their consumption pattern and lifestyle than in the poor part of the world. The concept of an ecological footprint contains the idea of equality and the obligation of the citizens in the rich part of the world to reduce consumption and waste. Dobson does not extend his concept of ecological citizenship as far as to include a basic income, though it may be seen as a natural consequence of his theory on ecological citizenship.

This connection is brought to light by the Italian Giunluca Busilacchi who talks about: 'Two problems, One Solution: Earth Basic Income' (Paper, BIEN Congress, 2004). The method for implementing a global basic income is to combine it with a global eco-tax on the ecological footprint. The overconsumption of the rich countries appears as a large ecological footprint, and the underconsumption of the poor countries appears as poverty: a small ecological footprint. A basic income in the poor part of the world may be part of a solution to the poverty problems, while an eco-tax and a basic income in the rich part of the world may be an element in the solution to the pollution and overconsumption problems, the eco-tax being part of the financial basis for the global basic income.

Another way of imagining a global basic income is in the form of a dividend. The Dutch, René Heeskens, who founded 'Global Basic Income Foundation', (http://www.globalincome.org/) proposes an Earth Dividend. His premises are that we have a common equal property right to the earth. In his model a dividend of this common property, Earth Dividend, is not given by the state or other international institutions to the citizens and is not founded on taxes. It could, however, be founded on the income all world citizens receive when they rent out their right to nature (quota) to companies and states, with the condition that these personal quotas may not be bought or sold. In practice, the sales with quotas must be transacted by independent funds (such as pension funds) which should secure all an equal cash payment of the dividend. Such a model of a common dividend fund is already realised in Alaska through The Alaska Permanent Fund where all citizens since 1982 every year receive a dividend (between 1000 and 2000 dollars) based on the revenues from the resources of the state. The Dutch philosopher Wouter Achterberg (1999) supports the idea of an ecological footprint and says that the abstract concept of equality behind the arguments for a basic income is compatible with the core in the concept of strong sustainability. Achterberg uses an argument for treating man equally in the distribution of natural resources which goes back to Thomas Paine's idea about all people having a property right to the earth. On this basis he establishes a resource-equity principle after St. Luper-Foy (1995) which says that the resources should be distributed equally among the current and the future generations, unless good reasons for an unequal distribution may be given. This resource-equity principle may be generalised to a sustainable consumption-production principle: Each generation may consume natural resources, pollute, and reproduce at given rates only if it could reasonably expect that each successive generation could do likewise. With this reasoning Achterberg may conclude that both a basic income and strong sustainability can be ethically justified and that there is a substantial ethical convergence between their justifications. Or, as he says, that an introduction of a basic income would contribute substantially to making the welfare state green.

Conclusion

As emphasised in the introduction, a basic income may be normatively argued for in various ways. It may be argued for from the perspectives of freedom, democracy or equity-distribution. In this article, I have, on the basis of Herman Daly's steady state paradigm, argued that the justice dimension is central, and that the global perspective is important. What this means is that basic income, which is in general only considered a fund, must also be regarded as a material, physical entity, to be respected and kept within global sustainable limits.

Therefore I will now, in concluding, argue for the existence of a specific normative order in the argumentation for a basic income in such a way that the global justice perspective must form the overall frame for all basic income considerations. Within this perspective of global sustainability, it is possible to construct a democratic perspective as a scope. Within the democratic scope, more specific forms of arguments may be developed, arguments connected to problems of the welfare state. One may be freedom in relation to the market, negatively understood as freedom from wage work and positively as the possibility for a wage for artists. It may also be expressed as a freedom to operate on the market, such as a freedom to manage one's capital and establish one's own company (support for entrepreneurs). Furthermore, it may be expressed as a freedom to create the production of subsistence, in other words capital goods to create an alternative economy. And finally, it may be expressed as a freedom in relation to the market, the state and the civil society.

I have previously argued that the idea of a basic income works on different dimensions (Christensen 2000C: 200-201): It may be viewed as: 1) an factor in setting limits to the use of nature, 2) a factor in setting a new limit to the commodification of labour, 3) a factor in setting a limit to clientisation in relation to the state, 4) a development of the citizenship, 5) a factor in creating a new gender balance, 6) an allocation of property rights which could be the foundation for a just market society.

One element in this argumentation was also that basic income may be seen in the light of various types of greater or smaller stories (ibid: 205-206): 1) as a global story about sustainable development and the good society, 2) as a great story about the development of democracy, citizenship and the welfare state, 3) as a couple of small stories about the problems of the welfare state (unemployment, clientisation, gender inequality), 4) as a number of technical stories about simplification and rationalisation of the system of transfer payment.

What is a story? A story tells a narrative about some actors acting on a scene. A story runs through some phases, it has a point and a conclusion. It distributes blame and responsibility, it carries a meaning and a possibility for identification for the actors. It is the narratives in a text (theory) which create coherence and totality in a frame. Like in my earlier argumentation, I think that the idea of sustainable development may bind together the six dimensions listed above (ibid: 467-469). The strength in the narrative of a sustainable development is precisely that it may function as a narrative framework for the smaller stories of basic income as a development of the social citizenship, as greater autonomy in relation to the state, the market and the civil society, and for the technical stories about rationalisation of the transfer system, the abolishment of poverty traps and the development of employment for the weak groups. There is not necessarily a contradiction between the small stories about basic income and the great one. On the contrary, the small story is strengthened by its relation to a greater story, and the greater story may also be strengthened by being put into practice in the small story.

BASIC INCOME ON THE POLITICAL AGENDA: BETWEEN INCLUSION AND EXCLUSION

In Denmark basic income has been on the political agenda twice since the idea was introduced with the book *Revolt from the Center* (*Oprør fra midten*) in 1978. The first time was in the beginning of the 1980s, and the second time was in the beginning of the 1990s. Except for this, basic income has not been an issue on the political agenda. But what does it mean to be on the political agenda, and how can a political movement act in such situations?

BACKGROUND

The book *Revolt from the Center* was such a success (in a few years it was published in over 100.000 copies) that the authors decided to form a new grass root movement 'The Revolt from the Center Movement' ('Midteroprøret') which in the beginning had some support (about 5000 subscribers to their periodical). The founders were surprised that the most popular element in their utopia was the idea of a basic income. It gave rise to the organisation of conferences and the publishing of a book about basic income (*Borgerløn og beskæftigelse*). In this way basic income was put on the political agenda by a number of opinion formers, and leading politicians from The Social Liberal Party (Det Radikale Venstre), The Socialist Peoples Party (Socialistisk Folkeparti) and The Social Democratic Party (Socialdemokratiet) were interested and sympathetic to the idea as being a way for a future society to be taken seriously.

In the late 1980s the The Revolt from the Center Movement lost its support, and the basic income idea disappeared from the political agenda. However, the idea returned to the political agenda in the 1990s, particularly in 1992-1994, though with new actors on the scene. Among those were people who had been excluded from the labour market together with outsiders in the labour market system (among trade unions and employers) and members in some political parties The Social Liberal Party (Det radikale Venstre), The Socialist Peoples Party (Socialistisk Folkeparti), The Christian Peoples Party (Kristeligt Folkeparti), Denmark's Liberal Party (Venstre) and The Unity List – the Red-Greens (Enhedslisten). Thus the subject was debated on national congresses of several parties, in the Social Commission, and in a special report from the Ministry of Economic Affairs.

Since 1995, when the rate of unemployment (12%) dropped, basic income has not been on the political agenda. Even though the *Danish Basic Income Movement*, which was founded in 2000, on several occasions has made an effort to put the question on the political agenda, it has not been successful in creating a general debate in which both political parties and opinion formers would participate.

WHAT DOES IT MEAN TO BE EXCLUDED?

Today basic income is far away from the dominating political agenda; it is excluded. The dominating political agenda tells that the welfare society needs reforms because of a change in the age distribution in the population. It needs to increase the labour supply and the employment and target the welfare services to the groups who have most needs. The main political trend points to a reduction in transfer payments, an increase in control, and a tightening up of the work obligation.

Against this agenda, The Basic Income Movement comes with their demands: 1) instead of targeting the transfer payments to the weakest, they propose to rationalise them and make them more universal, in line with a universal basic income, 2) instead of reducing the transfer payments in order 'to make it pay to work', they propose to remove the rules for deduction and move towards a universal basic income so that it would always pay to work, 3) instead of increasing the control, they propose that jobs (or activation) are offered as a free choice, 4) instead of emphasising the obligation to work, they emphasise the establishing of a new basic right to an income as an element in strengthening the citizenship.

The emphasis on work, control, reduction and obligation to work in the dominating political agenda stands in a striking contrast to the broader definition of work and activity, the free choice, the increased security and the new right to a basic income of the Basic Income Movement.

People who try to express ideas in opposition to the dominating political agenda often find it hard to penetrate to the public with articles and letters to the editors in the newspapers. They are not taken seriously, but rather considered 'theoretical', 'unrealistic', 'irresponsible', and 'utopian'. Such words are the rhetorical mechanisms of exclusion which The Basic Income Movement are often met with. Because of this, the concept of basic income is often one of negative stigmatisation. If you want to outdistance a political actor, you may tell him that his views resemble those of basic income, and in this way he will be stigmatised as 'irresponsible' or completely 'unrealistic'.

THE TENDENCY TO BE INCLUDED

On the other hand, to be taken seriously in the public opinion, it is necessary to show 'responsibility', 'pragmatism' and a willingness to compromise and accept the economy experts' description of the welfare problems.

If for a long time someone has experienced exclusion from the dominating political public, he will be marked by this 'stigmatisation'. He may feel that his opinion on basic income maybe is 'too much', or, at the moment, somewhat 'unrealistic'. He starts thinking, why maintain the concept 'basic income' when we are not winning acceptance for our message?

So if a person who speaks in favour of basic income wants to be in touch with the dominating public opinion and perhaps find allies who are not actual supporters of basic income, he will naturally try to adapt to their agenda to make the message of basic income less radical and more acceptable.

A possible outcome of this may be that he would think it better to talk about a 'participation income', new kinds of leaves, ticket coupons, an alternative labour market and an improvement of the activation system, rather than upholding the pure model of basic income. Are we not getting further by forming an alliance with the actors who are working for such arrangements that look like basic income, rather than sticking to basic income in its original pristine form?

THE TENDENCY TO BE EXCLUDED

Another reaction to the trouble of winning acceptance in the public with the pure message of basic income is that basic income is a topic 'too small' to set another agenda or to establish contact with groups who want to break away from the dominating agenda. The problem is that no one will be convinced by an isolated basic income reform if he is already engaged in a reform of the entire system. The basic income reform even points in different directions. Basic income is only part of the change. It will first be a convincing reform if it works together with other reforms. In a liberal political system it must be connected with privatisation and more radical tax reforms. In a socialist system it must be connected with other elements in a reform for economic democracy, and, finally, in a human ecological system it must be connected with an ecological tax reform and other ecological experiments.

THE DANGER OF INCLUSION AND OF FURTHER EXCLUSION

It is only natural, necessary and legitimate to get in touch with groups who, to some extent, sympathise with the idea of basic income, but who can not support the pure basic income idea. However, the Basic Income Movement is in danger of losing its identity if the adherents of basic income, in an effort to cooperate with these people, downplay the importance of the pure basic income model as a goal and end up patching up the existing system in various ways while avoiding talking about basic income. On the other hand, there is also a danger in trying to provide the Basic Income Movement with a broader goal, i.e. by creating a broader political programme for an alternative movement in which basic income is only one element. It may give rise to disagreement about ecology, EU, immigration policy and the attitude to capitalism with the result that the cross-party character of the movement must be dropped. This may lead to a situation where it is even more difficult for the movement to be heard and further exclusion would seem inevitable.

WHAT TO DO?

The ideal for a social movement wanting to change the system is to be placed in a position where it is neither included nor excluded. In such a position it is part of the political agenda without being seized by the dominating trend. It has connections and alliances with actors in the system while at the same time contradicting the system at critical points. This is the message from the Norwegian law philosopher Thomas Mathiesen in the book *Makt og Modmakt* (Pax 1982). By being put in a position both inside and outside of the system, it is possible for the movement to move and change the system, while it is powerless when it is either included or excluded.

The ongoing and crucial task for the Basic Income Movement is to break with the dualistic approach which the dominating political agenda uses to neutralise and eliminate competing views. Either you support the premises of the dominating perception, and you are considered 'responsible', 'pragmatic', 'supportive of short-term reforms' and 'compromise-seeking', or you are 'irresponsible', 'theoretical', 'utopian' and prepare the ground for fundamental changes of the system.

Basic income is fascinating as a subject because, on the whole, it moves away from this dualistic perception. It is linked to a number of practical problems and to great reforms. It represents a continuation of elements in the existing system and a discontinuation of other tendencies. It is concerned with short term questions while also having long term perspectives. It concurs with certain elements of the existing welfare system and not with others.

In other words, basic income must, to be able to transcend the dualistic view, be both 'realistic' and 'utopian' in the sense that it must show how it might be implemented within a realistic time horizon and with realistic costs while also being an expression of a new conception of justice which may do away with the injustice that is a part of the existing system. Basic income is economically feasible and a logical continuation of the current system (various forms of leave, transition payment, old age pension, early retirement benefit), but it also represents a big step away from some of the most prevalent features of the system (forced activation and the duty to work).

It may be argued that basic income paves the way for a new and expanded freedom for all citizens because it is connected with the citizenship. It is a real freedom in the sense that it is a combination of a negative freedom (from material shortage and from control) and a positive freedom (opportunities for making genuine free choices). This freedom works on different dimensions. It is a freedom in relation to the market because, on the one hand, with a basic income no one is forced to sell his labour power, and on the other, anyone will be in a better position to sell his labour power or be self-employed. In relation to the state, the basic income sets people free by doing away with the duty to work and the clientisation. And, finally, in relation to the family, it will secure economic independence between husband and wife and between children and parents, while in the civil society it will give people enough spare time for participation in the political life. All in all, it will constitute a substantial democratic renewal.

In the future, a principal argument for basic income must therefore be that it is an important element in the development of our democracy. In Denmark it is popular to motivate political actions with the reason that 'it will strengthen the social cohesion'. This may be another word for democracy.

Exactly this is an important future task for the Basic Income Movement: to argue that basic income is an important element in the process of strengthening the cohesion of society. The welfare society is moving towards a pure wage work society which is why there is an urgent need to establish a new democratic right, a right to a basic income that will change it to a real society for citizens.

REFERENCES

Abrahamson, Peter (1998) 'Efter velfærdsstaten: Ret og pligt til aktivering'. *Nordisk Socialt Arbeid.* Vol.18. Nr. 3, pp. 133-143.

Achterberg, Wouter (1999) 'From sustainability to basic income' in Michael Kenny and James Meadowcroft (Eds.) *Planning Sustainability,* London and New York: Routledge, pp. 128-147.

Adler-Karlsson, Gunnar (1976) *Lærebog for 80'erne. Et antikonsumistisk manifest,* København: Fremads Fokusbøger.

Adler-Karlsson, Gunnar (1977) *Nej til fuld beskæftigelse – ja til materiel grundtryghed,* København: Erling Olsens Forlag.

Andersen, Bent Rold (1984) *Kan vi bevare velfærdsstaten?* København: AKF's Forlag, pp. 133-211.

Andersen, Bent Rold (1996) 'Samfundsøkonomi, beskæftigelse og socialpolitik'. In Esben Dalgaard et al. (red.) *Velfærdsstatens fremtid.* København: Handelshøjskolens Forlag, pp. 133-211.

Andersen, Jørgen Goul (1995) 'Arbejdsløshed, polarisering og solidaritet'. *Social Politik* nr. 4, pp. 5-15.

Andersen, Jørgen Goul (2004) 'Danskernes opbakning til velfærdsstaten – urokkelig, påvirkelig eller skrøbelig?' in Jørn Henrik Petersen & Klaus Petersen (red): *13 udfordringer til den danske velfærdsstat.* Odense. Syddansk Universitetsforlag, pp. 117-128.

Basic Income Earth Network, http://www.econ.ucl.ac.be/ETES/BIEN/

Borchorst, Anette (1998) 'Køn, velfærdsstatsmodeller og familiepolitik', in Jørgen Elm Larsen & Iver Hornemann Møller (eds.) *Socialpolitik.* Viborg: Munksgaard, pp. 122-151.

Borgerlønsbevægelsen (The Basic Income Movement), http://www.borgerloen.dk/

Brittan, Samuel (1995), *Capitalism with a Human Face*, Aldershot: Edward Elgar.

Busilacchi, Gianluca (2004) 'Two Problems, One Solution: The Earth Basic Income'. BIEN 10th Bi-annual Congress, 19–20 September 2004, Barcelona. www.etes.ucl.ac.be/bien/Resources/Congress2004.htm

Callesen, Gerd and Hans Norbert Lahme (1978) *Den danske arbejderbevægelses programmatiske dokumenter og love (1871 til 1913)*. Odense: Odense Universitetsforlag.

Carlsen, Søren and Larsen, Jørgen Elm (eds.) (1994) *The Equality Dilemma. Reconciling Working Life and Family Life, Viewed from an Equality Perspective – the Danish Example*. Copenhagen: Munksgaard.

Carstens, Anette (1998) *Aktivering – klientsamtaler og socialpolitik*. København: Hans Reitzels Forlag.

Christensen, Ann-Dorte og Birte Siim (2001) *Køn, Demokrati og Modernitet. Mod nye politiske identiteter*. Gylling: Hans Reitzels Forlag.

Christensen, Erik (1998) 'Citizen's income as a heretical, political discourse: the Danish debate about citizen's income', Working paper from the Department of Economics, Politics and Public Administration, Aalborg University, 1998: 2. 18 p.

Christensen, Erik (1999) 'Citizen's income as a heretical, political discourse: the Danish debate about citizen's income' in Jens Lind, Iver Hornemann Møller (eds.) *Inclusion and Exclusion: Unemployment and Non-standard Employment in Europe*. Aldershot: Ashgate, pp. 13-33.

Christensen, Erik (2000A) 'The Rhetoric of »Rights and Obligations« in »Workfare« and »Citizens' Income« Paradigms/Discourses in Denmark in a Labour History Perspective'. Paper presented at the 8th International Congress on Basic Income, Berlin, October 6-7, 2000

Christensen, Erik (2000B) 'Ret og pligt i velfærdsstaten'. In Claus Clausen og Haakon Lærum (red.) *Velfærdsstaten i krise. En antologi*. København: Tiderne Skifter, pp. 26-39.

Christensen, Erik (2000C) *Borgerløn. Fortællinger om en politisk idé*. Århus: Hovedland.

Christensen, Erik (2001) 'The Rhetoric of »Rights and Obligations« in »Workfare« and »Citizens' Income« Paradigms/Discourses in Denmark in a Labour History Perspective'. Working paper from the Department of Economics, Politics and Public Administration, Aalborg University, 2001:3. 17 p.

Christensen, Erik (2002) 'Feminist Arguments in Favour of Welfare and Basic Income in Denmark.' Paper presented at the 9th International Congress on Basic Income. Geneva September 12-14, 2002.

Christensen, Erik (2003) 'Feminist Arguments in Favour of Welfare and Basic Income in Denmark.' Working paper from the Department of Economics, Politics and Public Administration, Aalborg University 2003: 2. 24 p.

Christensen, Erik (2004A) 'Welfare Discourses in Denmark seen in a Basic Income Perspective'. Paper presented at the 10th International Congress on Basic Income, Barcelona, September 19 -21, 2004.

Christensen, Erik (2004B) 'Feminist Arguments in Favour of Welfare and Basic Income in Denmark.', in Guy Standing (ed.) *Promoting Income Security as a Right: Europe and North America*. London: Anthem Press, pp. 382-400.

Christensen, Erik (red.) (2004C) *Velfærd på vildspor. Modsigelser i velfærdssamfundet*. København: Frydenlund.

Christensen, Erik (2005) 'Welfare Discourses in Denmark seen in a Basic Income Perspective'.Working paper from the Department of Economics, Politics and Public Administration, Aalborg University, 2005:7. 31 p.

Christensen, Erik and Loftager, Jørn (2000) 'Ups and Downs of Basic Income in Denmark.', in *Basic Income on the Agenda : Policy objectives and political chances*, Robert van der Veen and Loek Groot, (Eds.), Amsterdam, The Netherlands : Amsterdam University Press, pp. 257-268

Christensen, Erik, Karsten Lieberkind og Christian Ydesen (red.) (2007) *Retten til Basisindkomst. En demokratisk frigørelse*. Göteborg: NSU Press.

Dahl, Tove Stang (ed.) (1985) *Kvinnerett I og II*. Oslo: Universitetsforlaget AS.

Dahl, Tove Stang (1987) *Women's Law. An Introduction to Feminist Jurisprudence.* Oslo: Norwegian University Press.

Daly, Herman E. (1968) 'On Economics as a Life Science'. *Journal of Political Economy*, vol. 76, pp. 392–406.

Daly, Herman E. (ed.) (1973) *Steady-State Economy*, San Francisco: W.H. Freeman and Company, Vol. 6, Dec., pp. 185-193.

Daly, Herman E. (1977) *Steady-State Economics. The Economics of Biophysical Equilibrium and Moral Growth.* San Francisco: W.H. Freeman and Company.

Daly, Herman E. & John B. Cobb, Jr. (1990) *For the Common Good. Redirecting the Economy towards Community, the Environment and a Sustainable Future.* London: Green Print.

Daly, Herman E. (1992) 'Allocation, distribution, and scale: towards an economics that is efficient, just and sustainable' in *Ecological Economics*, Vol.6, Dec. pp. 185–193.

Daly, Herman E. (1996) *Beyond Growth. The Economics of Sustainable Development.* Boston: Beacon Press.

Dobson, Andrew (2003) *Citizenship and the Environment.* Oxford: Oxford University Press.

Engelbreth Larsen, Rune (red.) (2002) *Oprør fra bredden. Fra velfærdsstat til borgerløn.* København: Tiderne Skifter.

Esping-Andersen, Gøsta (1990) *The Three Worlds of Welfare Capitalism.* Oxford: Polity Press.

Fairclough, Norman (1992) *Discourse and Social Change.* Cambridge: Polity press.

Foss, Sonja K. (1996) *Rhetorical Criticism. Exploration & Practice.* Second Edition. Illinois: Waveland press.

Fraser, Nancy (1993) 'Clintonism, Welfare, and Antisocial Wage: The Emergence of a Neoliberal Political Imaginary'. *Rethinking Marxism* Vol. 6. No. 1 (Spring), pp. 10-23.

Fraser, Nancy (1994) 'After the Family Wage. Gender Equity and the Welfare State'. *Political Theory*, Vol. 22. No.4, pp. 591-618.

Fraser, Nancy (1997) *Justice Interruptus. Critical Reflections on the 'Postsocialist' Condition*. New York & London: Routledge.

Fraser, Nancy & Linda Gordon (1994) "Dependency' Demystified: Inscriptions of Power in a Keyword of the Welfare State'. *Social Policy*. Spring, pp. 4-30.

Friedman, Milton (1962) *Capitalism and Freedom*. Chicago: University of Chicago Press.

Giddens, Anthony (1994) *Beyond Left and Right*. Cambridge: Polity Press.

Giddens, Anthony (1998) *The Third Way. The Renewal of Social Democracy*. Oxford: Polity Press.

Gorz, André. (1979) 'Økologi og frihed', Viborg: *Politisk Revy* [English edition, *Ecology as Politics*, London: Pluto Press 1983].

Gorz, André (1981) 'Farvel til Proletariatet – hinsides socialismen', Viborg: *Politisk Revy* [English edition, *Farewell to Working Class: an Essay on Post-industrial Socialism*, London: Pluto Press 1982].

Gorz. André (1983) 'Paradisets veje – kapitalens dødskamp', Viborg: *Politisk Revy* [English edition, *Path to Paradise: on the Liberation from Work*, London: Pluto Press 1985].

Goul Andersen, Jørgen & Christian Albrekt Larsen (2008) 'How ideas can have an independent causal effect on policy change: The case of new economic ideas that changed the Danish welfare state'. Paper prepared for the 4th International Conference on Welfare State Change: Policy Feedback, the Role of Ideas and Incrementalism at St. Restrup Herregaard, Denmark, January 30 – February 1, 2008.

Goul Andersen, Jørgen & Jacob J. Pedersen (2007) 'Continuity and change in Danish active labour market policy: 1990-2007. The battlefield between activation and workfare'. CCWS Working Paper no. 2007-54.

Gouldner, Alvin W. (1955) 'Metaphysical pathos and the theory of bureaucracy'. *American Political Science Review*, 49, pp. 496-507.

Gouldner, Alvin W. (1960) 'The Norm of Reciprocity. A Preliminary Statement'. *American Sociological Review.* 25: 161-178 in *For Sociology. Renewal and Critique in Sociology Today*. New York: Basic Books. Inc. Publ. 1973, pp. 226-259.

Gouldner, Alvin W. (1970 and 1977, 2nd ed.) *The Coming Crises of Western Sociology*. London: Heinemann.

Gouldner, Alvin W. (1973) 'The Importance of Something for Nothing' in *For Sociology: Renewal and Critique in Sociology Today*. New York: Basic Books. Inc. Publ. 1973, pp. 260-299.

Green-Pedersen, Christoffer; Baggesen Klitgaard, Michael; Sonne Nørgaard, Asbjørn (2004) *Den danske velfærdsstat: Politiske, sociologiske og institutionelle dynamikker – En rapport til velfærdskommissionen*. www.velfaerd.dk.

Habermas, Jürgen (1996) *Between Facts and Norms. Contribution to Discourse Theory of Law and Democracy*, Cambridge: Polity Press.

Hall, Peter (1993) 'Policy Paradigms, Social Learning, and the State: The Case of Economic Policymaking in Britain', *Comparative Politics*, vol. 25(3), pp. 275-96.

Hansen, Henning, Jens Lind og Iver Hornemann Møller (2000) 'To work or not to work – that is not the question in the state of Denmark'. Paper.

Heeskens, René (2005) 'Earth Dividend and Global Basic Income: A Promising Partnership'. http://www.globalincome.org/English/Earth-Dividend.html.

Hirschman, Albert O. (1991) *The Rhetoric of Reaction. Perversity, Futility, Jeopardy*, Cambridge: The Belknap Press of Harvard University Press.

Hoff, Niels (1983) *Borgerstipendiet – den liberale velfærdsmodel*. Forlaget i Haarby.

Højgaard, Lis (1994) 'Work and Family – Life's Inseparable Pair' in Carlsen, Søren and Larsen Jørgen Elm (eds.) (1994) *The Equality Dilemma. Reconciling Working Life and Family Life, Viewed from an Equality Perspective – the Danish Example*. Copenhagen: Munksgaard, pp. 15-28.

Jamieson, Kathleen Hall (1995) *Beyond the Double Bind. Women and Leadership*. Oxford: Oxford University Press.

Jensen, Per H. (1999) 'Activation of the unemployed in Denmark since the early 1990s. Welfare or Workfare?' CCWS Working paper no. 1/1999. Department of Economics, Politics and Public Administration. Aalborg University.

Jensen, Per H. (2000) 'The Danish leave-of-absence schemes. Origins, functioning and effects from a gender perspective'. CCWS Working paper no. 2000-19. Center for Comparative Welfare State Studies. Department of Economics, Politics and Public Administration. Aalborg University.

Jessop, Bob (1995) 'Towards a Schumpeterian Workfare Regime in Britain? Reflections on Regulation, Governance, and Welfare State', *Environment and Planning* 27 (11), pp. 1613-26.

Jordan, Bill (1992) 'Basic Income and the Common Good', in Philippe Van Parijs (ed.) *Arguing for Basic Income*, London and New York: Verso, pp. 155-177.

Jørgensen, Henning; Bredgaard, Thomas; Dalsgaard, Lene og Larsen, Flemming (red.). (2002) *Arbejde og politik – undervejs med CARMA*. Aalborg Universitet.

Ketscher, Kirsten (1990) *Offentlig børnepasning i retlig belysning,* Gylling: Jurist og Økonomforbundets Forlag.

Ketscher, Kirsten (1995) 'Offentlig og privat i socialretten' in Lin Adrian et al. (eds.) *Ret & Privatisering*, København: GadJura, pp. 137-158.

Ketscher, Kirsten (2001) 'From Marriage Contract to Labour Contract, Effects on Care Duties and Care Rights' in Kevät Nousiainen (ed.) *Responsible Selves. Women in the Nordic Legal Culture*. Dartmouth: Ashgate, pp. 155-173.

Ketscher, Kirsten (2002A) 'The Danish Social Welfare System' in Børge Dahl, Torben Melchior, Ditlev Tamm (eds.) *Danish Law in a European Perspective*. 2nd Edition: Copenhagen: Thomson Publishers, pp. 299-318.

Ketscher, Kirsten (2002B) *Socialret*. 2. udg. Århus: Forlaget Thomson. Gad Jura.

Korpi, Walter & Joakim Palme (1998) 'The Paradox of Redistribution and Strategies of Equality: Welfare State Institutions, Inequality, and Poverty in the Western Countries', *American Sociological Review*, 63, 3, pp. 661-687.

Kuhn, Thomas S. (1962) *The Structure of Scientific Revolutions*, Chicago: University of Chicago Press.

Kærgård, Niels (1997) 'Den danske socialpolitiske forskningstradition'. *Nationaløkonomisk Tidsskrift*, 135, pp. 199-210

Laclau, Ernesto and Mouffe, Chantall (1985) *Hegemony and Socialist Strategy*. London: Verso.

Larsen, Christian Albrekt (2008) 'The Institutional Logic of welfare Attitudes;: How Welfare Regimes Influence Public Support'. *Comparative Political Studies*. Vol 41, No. 2, February 2008, pp. 145-168.

Lewis, Jane (2001) 'The Decline of the Male Breadwinner Model: Implications for Work and Care'. *Social Politics* vol 8 (1), pp. 152-181.

Lewis, Jane and Ilona Ostner (1994) 'Gender and the Evolution of European Social Policies'. Centre for Social policy Research, University of Bremen. ZeS-Arbeitspaier Nr. 4/94.

Lind, Jens and Iver Hornemann Møller (eds.) (1999) *Inclusion and Exclusion: Unemployment and Non-standard Employment in Europe*. London: Ashgate.

Lindbeck, A., S. Nyberg and J. W. Weibull (1999) 'Social Norms and Economic Incentives in the Welfare State', *Quarterly Journal of Economics*, 114(1), pp 1-37.

Lister, Ruth (1995) 'Dilemmas in engendering citizenship', *Economy and Society*, 24 (1), pp. 1-40.

Loftager, Jørn (1998) 'Solidarity and Universality in the Danish Welfare State – empirical remarks and theoretical interpretations'. BIEN International Congress 1998. Amsterdam, 10-12. sept. 1998.

Loftager, Jørn (1999) *Aktivering eller medborgerskab. Nå, hvad laver du så? Om arbejde, arbejdsløshed og kvalifikationer i det 21. århundrede – et debatskrift i anledning af Magistrenes Arbejdsløshedskasses 25 års jubilæum*. Magistrenes Arbejdsløshedskasse, pp. 62-70.

Loftager, Jørn (2002) 'Deliberative Democracy and The Legitimacy of Basic Income'. Paper for the 9th International Congress of Basic Income European Network. ILO 12-14 sept. 2002.

Luper-Foy, St. (1995) 'International justice and the environment' i D. Cooper and J. Palmer (Eds.) *Just Environments*, London: Routledge, pp. 91-117.

Marshall, Thomas H. (1950) *Class, Citizenship and the State*. Cambridge: Cambridge University Press.

Mathiesen, Thomas (1982) *Makt og Motmakt*, Oslo: Pax.

Mathiesen, Thomas (1992), *Det uferdige. Tekster om opprør og undertrykkelse*, Oslo: Pax Forlag.

McKay, Alisa (2001) 'Rethinking Work and Income Maintenance Policy: Promoting Gender Equality Through a Citizens' Basic Income'. *Feminist Economics* 7(1), pp. 97-118.

McKay, Alisa and Jo Vanevery (2000) 'Gender, Family, and Income Maintenance: A Feminist Case for Citizens Basic Income'. *Social Politics*, Summer, pp. 266-284.

Meyer, Niels I., Kristen Helveg Petersen, Villy Sørensen (1978), *Oprør fra midten*, København: Gyldendal.

Meyer, Niels I., Kristen Helveg Petersen, Villy Sørensen (1982), *Røret om oprøret. Mere om midten*, København: Gyldendal.

Meyer, Niels I., Kristen Helveg Petersen, Villy Sørensen (1982) *Revolt from the Centre*, London: Maryon Boyars.

Offe, Claus (1984) *Contradictions of the Welfare State*. Cambridge, Massachusetts: The MIT Press.

Offe, Claus (1992) 'A Non-Productivist Design for Social Policies', in Phillippe van Parijs (ed.) *Arguing for Basic Income. Ethical Foundations for Radical Reform*, London and New York: Verso, pp. 61-78.

Offe, Claus (1996) *Modernity & The State East West*. Cambridge: Polity Press.

Ostner, Ilona (1996) 'Individualization, Breadwinner Norms, and Family Obligations. Gender Sensitive Concepts in Comparative Welfare'. Feminist Research Centre in Aalborg. Paper December.

Pateman, Carole (1989) *The Disorder of Women. Democracy, Feminism and Political Theory*. Cambridge: Polity Press.

Petersen, Hanne (1994) 'Law and Order in Family Life and Working Life' in Carlsen, Søren and Larsen Jørgen Elm (eds.) (1994) *The Equality Dilemma. Reconciling Working Life and Family Life, Viewed from an Equality Perspective – the Danish Example*. Copenhagen: Munksgaard, pp. 41-52.

Petersen, Jørn Henrik (1996A) 'Værdier og interesser i socialpolitikken', *Politica* 28. årg. Nr. 4, pp. 440-452.

Petersen, Jørn Henrik (1996B) *Vandringer i Velfærdsstaten. 11 bidrag til velfærdsstatens legitimitet*. Gylling: Odense Universitetsforlag.

Petersen, Jørn Henrik & Klaus Petersen (red) (2004) *13 udfordringer til den danske velfærdsstat*. Odense. Syddansk Universitetsforlag.

Polanyi, Karl (1957) *The Great Transformation*. Reprint. Boston: Beacon.

Rhys-Williams, Juliet (1943) *Something to Look Forward to: A Suggestion for a New Social Contract*, London: MacDonald.

Scott, Joan W. (1988) 'Deconstructing equality versus difference: or the uses of poststructuralist theory for feminism', *Feminist Studies* 14 (1), pp. 33-50.

Siim, Birte (2000) *Gender and Citizenship. Politics and Agency in France, Britain and Denmark*. Cambridge: Cambridge University Press.

Siim, Birte (2001) 'How to Achieve Gender Equality?' Keynote Speech. Cost A 13 Conference. Social Policy, Marginalization and Citizenship. Aalborg University, Denmark, 2-4. November.

Socialdemokratiet (1995) *Velfærd med vilje*. Debatoplæg om Fremtidens velfærdssamfund.

Socialkommissionen (1993) *Reformer. Socialkommissionens samlede forslag*. København.

Standing, Guy (1999) *Global Labour Flexibility. Seeking Distributive Justice*. London: MacMillan.

Standing, Guy (2004) (ed.) *Promoting Income Security as a Right: Europe and North America*. London: Anthem Press.

Stigler, George J. (1946) The Economics of Minimum Wage Legislation, *The American Economic Review*, Vol. 36, No. 3, pp. 358-365

Torfing, Jacob (1999A) *New Theories of Discourse. Laclau, Mouffe and Zizek*. Oxford: Blackwell.

Torfing, Jacob (1999B) 'Workfare with Welfare: Recent reforms of the Danish Welfare State'. *Journal of European Social Policy* vol. 9 (1), pp. 5-28.

Torfing, Jakob (2000) 'Slaget er først lige begyndt'. *Tidsskriftet SALT*, nr. 5, Oktober, pp. 12-14.

Torfing, Jacob (2002) 'Aktivering, netværksstyring og terapeutiske reguleringsmåder'. *Samfundsøkonomen* nr. 7, pp. 33-40.

Velfærdskommissionen (2004) *Fremtidens velfærd kommer ikke af sig selv*. Maj 2004. www.velfaerd.dk

Wackernagel, Mathias and Rees, William E. (1996), *Our Ecological Footprint: Reducing Human Impact on the Earth*, British Columbia: New Society Publishers.

Weisskopf, Walter A. (1979) 'The Method is the Ideology: From a Newtonian to a Heisenbergian Paradigm in Economics', *Journal of Economic Issues*, vol. XIII. No. 4, pp. 869-884.

Wollstonecraft, Mary (1792/1997) *The Vindifications. The Rights of Men. The Rights of Women* (ed.) by D.L. Macddonald and Kathleen Scherf. Peterbourough: Broadview Press.

WWF (World Wildlife Fund) (2006) *Living Planet Report*.

ADDITIONAL LITERATURE IN ENGLISH RELEVANT TO THE BASIC INCOME DEBATE IN DENMARK

Andersen, Jørgen Goul (1996) 'Marginalisation, Citizenship and the Economy: The Capacity of The Universalist Welfare State in Denmark' in Erik Oddvar Eriksen and Jørn Loftager, (Eds.) *The Rationality of the Welfare State*, Oslo: Scandinavian University Press, pp. 155-202.

Andersen, Jørgen Goul (1997) 'The Scandinavian Welfare Model in Crisis? – Achievements and Problems of the Danish Welfare State in an Age of Unemployment and Low Growth'. *Scandinavian Political Studies*, vol. 20 no. 1, pp. 1-31.

Andersen, Jørgen Goul (1997) 'Beyond Retrenchment: Welfare Policies in Denmark in the 1990s'. Aalborg : Aalborg Universitet, *Arbejdspapirer fra Institut for Økonomi, Politik og Forvaltning*, no. 8.

Andersen, Jørgen Goul and Ole Borre (1997). 'Voting and Political Attitudes in Denmark'. Aarhus: *Aarhus University Press*. Chapter 7.

Andersen, Jørgen Goul (2002) 'Coping with Long-Term Unemployment: Economic security, labour Market Integration and Well-being. Results from a Danish Panel Study, 1994-1999'. *International Journal of Social Welfare*, vol. 11(2), pp. 178-190.

Andersen, Jørgen Goul (2002) 'Work and citizenship: Unemployment and unemployment policies in Denmark, 1980-2000', in Jørgen Goul Andersen and Per H. Jensen (Eds.) *Changing Labour Markets, Welfare Policies and Citizenship*, Bristol: Policy press, pp. 59-84.

Birnbaum, Simon and Erik Christensen (2007) Anthroposophical Reflections on Basic Income. Johannes Hohlenberg, *Basic Income Studies. An International Journal of Basic Income Research* Vol. 2, Issue 2, December.

Brun, Ellen (1994) 'The new social contract: sustainability from below.' Aalborg. Paper 18 p.

Brun, Ellen (2000) 'Conceptualizing a New Social Contract' in Johannes Dragsbæk-Schmidt and Jacques Hersh (Eds), *Globalization and Social Change*. London and New York: Routledge, pp. 267–282.

Brun, Ellen 'Expropriation and Reappropriation of the Means of Subsistence', in *Privatization and Development,* (eds.) Vibeke Andersson and Johannes Dragsbæk Schmidt, London: Zed Press (forthcoming)

Christensen, Erik (1998) 'An Analysis of the Danish Political Debate on Citizen's Income in the period 1977-97'. Paper presented at the 7th International Congress on basic Income, Amsterdam 10-12 Sept., 21 p.

Lind, Jens and Iver Hornemann Møller (1995) 'Unemployment or Basic Income – is there a Middle Road?', Copenhagen Business School. *CID Studies* no. 9.

Lind, Jens and Iver Hornemann Møller (1997) 'Unemployment Policy in Denmark', in *International Journal of Employment Studies,* Vol 5, No 1, Sydney, pp. 95-115.

Lind, Jens and Iver Hornemann Møller (1999) 'Unemployment or Basic Income? – Danish Debates', in Ian Gough and Gunnar Olufsson (Eds.), *Capitalism and social cohesion. Essays on Exclusion and Integration*, London: Macmillan, pp. 169-188.

Lind, Jens and Iver Hornemann Møller (2004) 'The Danish experience of labour market policy and activation of the unemployed', in Serrano, A. (Ed.), *Are Activation Policies Converging in Europe*, ETUI, Brussels, pp. 163-196.

Lind, Jens and Iver Hornemann Møller (2006) 'Activation for what purpose? Lessons from Denmark' *International Journal of Sociology and Social Policy*, Vol. 26 Issue, pp. 5-19.

Loftager, Jørn (1992) *Basic Income – an institutional Mechanism Beyond the Market-Welfare State Compromise?* Aarhus: Institute of Political Science.

Loftager, Jørn (1992) 'Basic income—an institutional mechanism beyond the market-welfare State compromise?' Paper presented at the workshop on The Politics of Civil Society and the Welfare State, University of Limerick, 30 March-4 April, 30 p.

Engelbreth Larsen, Rune (red.) (2002) *Oprør fra bredden. Fra velfærdsstat til borgerløn*. København: Tiderne Skrifter.

Gemynthe, Finn (1998) *Rigdom uden arbejde. Dovenskabens politik og godmodighedens styrke*. København: Christian Ejlers Forlag.

Hoff, Niels (1981) *Borgerstipendiet – den liberale velfærdsmodel*. Forlaget i Haarby.

Hornemann Møller, Iver, Jens Lind & Henning Hansen (2008) *Aktivering – Disciplinering til arbejde*. København: CASA.

Höglund, Mats: *Basinkomst, demokrati och ekonomisk-politisk realism*. Bokmanus. 2006.

Janson, Per (2003) *Den huvudlösa idén – Basinkomst, välfärdspolitik och en blockerad debatt*. Lund: Arkiv.

Jönsson, Bodil (1999) *Tio tankar om tid*. Stockholm: Brombergs Förlag.

Kildal, Nanna (red.) (2000) *Den nya sociala frågan. Om arbete, inkomst och rättvisa*. Göteborg: Daidalos.

Meyer, Niels I., Kristen Helveg Petersen og Villy Sørensen (1978) *Oprør fra midten*. København: Gyldendal.

Meyer, Niels I., Kristen Helveg Petersen og Villy Sørensen (1982) *Røret om oprøret. Mere om midten*. København: Gyldendal.

Morgenstierne, Syphilia (2000) *Elsk Deg Rig*. Nesbru: Forlaget Fritt og vilt.

Vennerød, Christian (1983) *Arbejdstid – levetid*. Århus: Husets Forlag 1983.

Øyen, Else (red.) (1981) *GMI. Garanteret Minsteinntekt i Norge*. Oslo: Universitetsforlaget.

Øyen, Else (red.) (1991) *Velferdsstaten. Den fornuftige samfunnsmodell*. Oslo: Tiden Norsk Forlag.

BOOKS ABOUT BASIC INCOME IN SCANDINAVIAN LANGUAGES

Adler-Karlsson Gunnar (1975) *Lärobok för 80-talet*. Stockholm: Prisma.

Adler-Karlsson, Gunnar (1976) *Lærebog for 80'erne. Et antikonsumistisk manifest*. København: Fremads Fokusbøger.

Adler-Karlsson, Gunnar (1977) *Nej til fuld beskæftigelse – ja til materiel grundtryghed*. København: Erling Olsens Forlag.

Adler-Karlsson, Gunnar (1990) *Lärobok för 90-talet*. Stockholm: Prisma

Andrup, Henrik (1983) *Lærebog for en eventuel næste generation*. Viborg: Hekla.

Borgerlønsgruppen (1983) *Borgerløn og Beskæftigelse*. København: Midteroprørets Informationscenters Forlag.

Brandberg, Åsa (red.) (2005) *Ragnarök eller världens chans – om hotade livsvillkor och nya möjligheter*. Munka Ljungby: Humanistiska Förlaget.

Christensen, Erik (2000) *Borgerløn. Fortællinger om en politisk idé*. Århus: Hovedland.

Christensen, Erik, Karsten Lieberkind og Christian Ydesen (red.) (2007) *Retten til Basisindkomst. En demokratisk frigørelse*. Göteborg: NSU Press.

Ekstrand, Lasse (1995) *Den befriade tiden. Om arbete och medborgarlön*. Göteborg: Bokförlaget Korpen.

Ekstrand, Lasse (1996) *Arbetets död och medborgarlön. En essä om det goda livet*. Göteborg: Bokförlaget Korpen.

Ekstrand, Lasse 2001 (1998)) *Varje människa en konstnär. Samhällsvisionären och livskonstnären Joseph Beuys*. Bokförlaget Korpen.

Engelbreth Larsen, Rune (red.) (2002) *Oprør fra bredden. Fra velfærdsstat til borgerløn.* København: Tiderne Skrifter.

Gemynthe, Finn (1998) *Rigdom uden arbejde. Dovenskabens politik og godmodighedens styrke.* København: Christian Ejlers Forlag.

Hoff, Niels (1981) *Borgerstipendiet – den liberale velfærdsmodel.* Forlaget i Haarby.

Hornemann Møller, Iver, Jens Lind & Henning Hansen (2008) *Aktivering – Disciplinering til arbejde.* København: CASA.

Höglund, Mats: *Basinkomst, demokrati och ekonomisk-politisk realism.* Bokmanus. 2006.

Janson, Per (2003) *Den huvudlösa idén – Basinkomst, välfärdspolitik och en blockerad debatt.* Lund: Arkiv.

Jönsson, Bodil (1999) *Tio tankar om tid.* Stockholm: Brombergs Förlag.

Kildal, Nanna (red.) (2000) *Den nya sociala frågan. Om arbete, inkomst och rättvisa.* Göteborg: Daidalos.

Meyer, Niels I., Kristen Helveg Petersen og Villy Sørensen (1978) *Oprør fra midten.* København: Gyldendal.

Meyer, Niels I., Kristen Helveg Petersen og Villy Sørensen (1982) *Røret om oprøret. Mere om midten.* København: Gyldendal.

Morgenstierne, Syphilia (2000) *Elsk Deg Rig.* Nesbru: Forlaget Fritt og vilt.

Vennerød, Christian (1983) *Arbejdstid – levetid.* Århus: Husets Forlag 1983.

Øyen, Else (red.) (1981) *GMI. Garanteret Minsteinntekt i Norge.* Oslo: Universitetsforlaget.

Øyen, Else (red.) (1991) *Velferdsstaten. Den fornuftige samfunnsmodell.* Oslo: Tiden Norsk Forlag.